LIBRARIES

This book is to be returned on o
It may be borrowed for a further

MANY LIBRARIES IN ESSEX HAVE
FACILITIES FOR EXHIBITIONS AND
MEETINGS — ENQUIRE AT YOUR
LOCAL LIBRARY FOR DETAILS

THE WORD
AND THE FLESH

A Play

by

ALICE WILLIAMS

SAMUEL FRENCH

LONDON

NEW YORK SYDNEY TORONTO HOLLYWOOD

GB 573 06010 X

THE WORD AND THE FLESH

First performed by the Adult Drama Group of the Denbighshire Technical College, Wrexham, at the Palace Theatre, Rhos, Near Wrexham, on 4th March 1969, with the following cast of characters:

Joseph of Arimathea	*David Evans*
Jacob-ben-Levi	*Philip Edwards*
Shadrach	*Peter Davies*
John	*Gerard McConway*
Jesus	*Robert Davies*
Thomas	*Osian Wyn Jones*
Judas	*Stephen Lyons*
Mary of Magdala	*Wendy Griffiths*
Salome	*Rowena Jenkins*
Miriam	*Susan Cartlidge*
Martha	*Glenys Davies*
Peter	*Edward Gittins*
Mary, mother of Jesus	*Hannah Cumming*
Caiaphas	*Joe Wilson*
Annas	*Philip Mason*
James	*Christopher Humbert*
1st Guard ⎱ Jewish soldiers, Temple Guards	*Raymond Williams*
2nd Guard ⎰	*Kelvin Roberts*
Girl	*Anne Williams*
Girl's Aunt	*Irene Hughes*
Man born blind	*Kerith Hughes*
Rachel, his mother	*Kathleen Humphries*
Lazarus	*Russell Evans*
Pilate	*Bryn Lloyd Jones*
Claudia, his wife	*June Rich*
Rufus ⎱	*Charles James*
Scipio ⎟ Roman Centurions	*Philip Edwards*
Flavius ⎟	*Kerith Hughes*
Proclus ⎰	*Kelvin Roberts*

Lighting by W. H. Harris
Produced by Alice Williams

Dedicated to my mother and father.

AUTHOR'S NOTE

If the character of Jesus is not infinitely strong and *tough*, the dominating personality is that of Judas, and this not only upsets the balance of the play but destroys its primary motivation—to depict the enormous strength, humour, and control of the human Jesus.

THE WORD AND THE FLESH

ACT I

There is introductory music as the audience comes in (Mozart's Requiem Mass in D). This is followed by Hebrew cantor music.

The stage is in darkness, and out of the darkness comes the sound of many voices; coming from all directions they gradually get louder . . .

Christ have mercy on us . . .
Christ have mercy on us . . .
We are blind . . . We are sick . . . We are unhappy . . .
My child is sick . . . My daughter is dying . . .
We are poor . . . We are ignorant, teach us! Heal us!
Unclean! Unclean! A leper and unclean!
Jesus have pity!

Voice of Jesus I will. You are clean.
Voice of Supplicant Blind! Blind! Pity the blind. Jesus of Nazareth, give me sight.
Voice of Jesus You believe I can do this? Receive your sight.
Voices of Supplicants { I am sick. / I am deaf. / I am paralysed.
Voice of Disciple In the name of Jesus of Nazareth.
Voices of Supplicants { We are mad. / We are miserable.
Voice of Disciple In the name of Jesus of Nazareth.
Voices of Supplicants (*rising in* { We are lame.
   despair and urgency) { We are deaf, dumb, diseased, blind.
Voice of Disciple In the name of Jesus of Nazareth.

The voices die away, and are replaced by an Eastern dance

SCENE 1

The CURTAIN rises on a blaze of lights and noise, colour and movement, in the house of Joseph of Arimathea, a wealthy Jew, greatly influenced by the Romans. A meal and an evening's entertainment is in progress. There are three large tables; the guests recline in the Roman fashion, on couches. In front of the tables on the floor, is a pile of cushions and rugs. A girl on the floor plays a lyre and hums or sings. Two others, scantily dressed, dance. In the centre of the table sits the host, Joseph; on each side of him two close friends, Jacob-ben-Levi and Shadrach. They occupy the centre table. On their left two men talk earnestly, John and Jesus. Facing them, on Joseph's right, Thomas and Judas. The tables are sufficiently long for it to be feasible that speakers are not necessarily heard by each other across the tables. All these men are young. The music and dancing end, everybody claps appreciatively and the dancers subside on to the cushions.

Joseph Now—more wine? Mary, if you're not too exhausted, more wine please.

Mary Magdalene rises again in a leisurely manner and saunters off, very aware of her own charms

Jacob (*he and Shadrach are drunk*) You've offered us . . . mixed bag today; dancing girls, and prophets!
Shadrach Joseph's tastes are universal, and universally recognized. He's a great man our Joseph, I like him—and I like his parties—any new fad, you'll find it here. (*Raises his cup, tries to rise, staggers*) To our host!
Thomas (*nodding towards Jesus. He, too, is a little drunk, so his manner is rather owlish and his speech careful*) Wouldn't call him a fad exactly.
Shadrach Of course he is—a craze . . . a fad . . . novelty . . . churns people up, people like to be churned up.
Jacob (*hearing the last bit, stirring himself out of his drunken stupor*) Churned up! Poor Shadrach . . . Shadrach sick!
Shadrach Not me, you fool! Him! (*Points at Jesus*)
Thomas Now, mate, watch it! He's my friend—mustn't talk about him.

Judas looks amused. Jesus and John still talk quietly but with animation.

Mary re-enters, she carries a jug of wine and goes first to Judas, then she works slowly round the men, filling up their cups

Mary (*to Judas*) You're very quiet; come on, drink up! We haven't seen you here before.
Judas (*courteous, but a bit uncomfortable*) I'm not very good at this sort of thing, I don't go out much.
Jacob Austerity's for old people . . . must enjoy yourself . . . young . . . duty to have good time. You're young, I'm young . . . Shadrach's young. Are you young, Shadrach?
Shadrach Very young . . . mere child.
Jacob Enjoy . . . self!
Judas I do enjoy myself. This way doesn't appeal to me very much.

Jesus hears latter part of conversation and now it is his turn to look amused. Judas continues to look uncomfortable. All except Judas, John, Jesus and Mary are very drunk

Mary We're very short of handsome boys.
Shadrach I . . . resent that . . .

Mary Well, we're used to you, dear, I mean *new* handsome boys. (*She speaks to one of the girls giggling on the cushions*) Salome, come and sit by this poor lonely boy.

Salome gets up, she is quite without inhibition and she perches herself on Judas's knee

Salome He's nice, isn't he? I want to sit here, not on the floor, put your arm round me nicely—(*reluctantly Judas does so and she snuggles up to him*)—there that's better . . . all cosy. (*She stares across at Jesus, then pokes Thomas in the ribs*) I like him; he's attractive. I'll meet him later tonight if he likes.
Thomas (*slurred speech*) Which one? Both friends . . . nice friends.
Salome That one on the end.
Shadrach That's the wizard . . . don't bother with wizards . . . Joseph's funny friend . . . does miracles, gets bunnies out of hats. (*Laughs at his own joke*)
Salome I like his face; he can work some miracles on me, I'd like that.

Jesus hears all this and smiles, not in the least put out. At this point Mary reaches Shadrach, who grabs her. She puts the jug on the table and he pulls her on to his knee

Shadrach Stay here, my lady. (*He whispers to her, she giggles, they pet brazenly*)
Salome (*to Judas*) Did you know Joseph a long time? (*She is pulling his ears, playing with his hair, etc., but getting no encouragement*)
Judas Our families are old friends. I only met him recently. I told him I don't like parties.
Salome Rude boy! . . . Don't say that again! (*Slaps him*)

The third girl Miriam, dumb and also drunk, looks up, giggling to herself

Miriam I'll help you—poor boy, he's shy. (*She sits between Judas and Thomas, beams at both*)
Thomas Go-way, don't like drunk girls! Only men got right to drink.

Jesus looks across at the group, Judas shrugs, Jesus smiles, Jacob decides to deliver a lecture somewhat spoilt by slurred speech

Jacob Trouble with you, you're under-educated, socially under-educated. Don't know right people. Fantastic time if know . . . right people.
Shadrach Good party last week . . . Brutus . . . breakfast at dawn, good old Brutus . . . lots of booze, good drinker—Brutus.
Judas (*very lofty and removing an arm from his neck*) Do you mean to say you fraternize socially with the Romans? (*Loud laughter greets this*)
Jacob Mary—tell him! (*Imitates Judas in a posh accent*) "Do you mean to say you fraternize socially with the Romans?" (*More loud laughter*)
Mary (*unashamed and pert*) You bet I do. They have very generous natures, not like you lot. Jews are so cautious with their money.
Salome So are Greeks. Give me Romans every time. (*She eyes an ornate bangle on her arm with much satisfaction and the girls laugh*)
Mary They really are marvellously kind. (*Rude noises, etc., from the men*)

Miriam (*naïvely*) Of course, they make you work for it. (*More roars from the men*)

Salome No, really! They are kind. Last week one of the officers gave me a horse.

Shadrach A what?

Salome A horse—you know—a horse!

Jacob What for?

Salome To ride, you fool. I just happened to mention that I used to ride every day when I was at home in Tiberias—Herod was a fat pig but he was very generous. Well, this officer said, "You shall have my horse", and he's a beauty, black, and wicked looking.

Thomas How big is he?

Salome Seventeen hands.

Thomas Too big—much too big—fall off—women shouldn't ride horses, don't like women ride horses.

Miriam I don't think you like women.

Thomas Don't like women . . . Don't like my wife. (*Hiccup!*)

Salome I call him Bucephalus.

Jesus Bucephalus was white.

Salome It doesn't matter, he wasn't more beautiful.

Joseph How did he explain its loss to the army?

Miriam Maybe it was his own, or maybe he said it ran away.

Joseph That's very likely. The finest cavalry officers in the world and one of them admits his horse ran away! (*More laughter*)

Miriam I never thought of asking for a horse.

Salome Well, you can't ride.

Miriam No, there is that.

Mary I never thought of it either and I do ride. They always give me feminine things—you know, perfume, jewellery—but it's an idea. I'd like a horse, and if you have to sell them they fetch a good price.

Shadrach (*fondling her*) I'll buy a horse, I'll buy twenty horses, all black! (*Mary returns his caresses vaguely; in the middle of these antics she sees Jesus looking at her, she looks away, but looks back again*)

Judas However low I sank, I'd take nothing from Romans.

Mary Then you would be a fool, my friend. They think money will buy anything, and it will. (*She and Jesus are still staring at each other. Suddenly she gets off Shadrach's knee and goes straight to him*) Do you want more wine? I didn't get as far as you.

Jesus Yes, please.

She takes the jug from the table, pours some for him and for John, then turns to go. Jesus takes hold of her hand

Stay here and talk to us. You've spent all the evening with them.

Mary (*flustered, unusually so for her*) Just a moment, I must refill this.

Mary goes out

John (*quite over-awed*) What a beauty!

Jesus Yes. I know her family.

John Has she got a family? I never think of girls like that having a family somehow.

Salome Don't talk so silly; of course we've got families.

Thomas (*pointing at Jesus and scowling*) How do you know her? Don't want to bother with women, trouble-makers.

Jacob (*offensive*) . . . too expensive for a prophet . . . should have thought. (*He belches*) Pardon me . . . (*He pats his stomach*) Wind!

Jesus (*across to Thomas*) She's the youngest daughter in the Bethany family. You know, Martha and Lazarus.

John (*astounded*) No! Do they—well, you know—do they know about her?

Jesus Yes—they know.

Shadrach (*very, very drunk*) She's a lovely girl, a lovely, lovely girl . . . going to marry her! (*He thumps the table*)

Jacob (*shocked out of his stupor*) You wouldn't . . . couldn't!

Shadrach (*very emphatic*) Yes . . . would . . . no more Romans . . . break her bloody neck.

Jacob (*like a drunken owl*) Can't do it . . . not done . . . nobody invite you anywhere . . . no one talk to you . . . terrible life . . . (*The girls look indignant*)

Salome I'd have you know some very classy types have offered to marry me.

Miriam They don't want to marry me, I must admit, but that's not to say I'm not as good as they are.

Salome No, it's because you're dumb.

Miriam It doesn't matter, I've got a very nice nature. My grandmother used to say, when the other kids teased me, "Never mind, Miriam, you've got a very nice nature", and that's very important, isn't it? (*She appeals to Jesus*)

Jesus Yes indeed. That's very important.

Mary comes back carrying the jug, which she puts down. She gives Shadrach a quick look and then deliberately sits next to Jesus

Joseph (*amused*) Well, old boy, she's transferred her affections, and doesn't he look pleased with himself? Even prophets admire a pretty woman.

Jesus Why not?

Jacob . . . present better than future, prophet . . . enjoy . . . present . . . future mightn't come!

Jesus I agree with you there.

Thomas I vouch for that. He always says, "Sufficient for the day is the evil in it, let tomorrow take care of itself."

Shadrach Mary! Come on back, sweetheart . . . he's no good . . . prophet's no good . . . holy man . . . no women . . . no wine . . . no life . . . no nothing!

Miriam (*earnestly*) I'm sure that's not true, about him being no good, I mean. I can always tell . . . just by looking at a man . . . he's tough that one. Anyway, he's a carpenter. Aren't you a carpenter?

Jesus I'm a carpenter.

Miriam Do you like women?

Jesus (*smiling*) Some women.

Miriam I'm glad. I bet they like you, too.

Thomas (*gloomily*) Always after him . . . damned nuisance . . .

Shadrach (*waving his cup around*) Have to get nasty . . . prophet make her come back . . . I know what to do with her . . . prophet's no good. (*There is laughter, but Shadrach is really nasty*) Mary! Here! Come on here!

Mary Be quiet, you're making a fool of yourself.

Shadrach (*pulls a knife out of his belt and advances on Mary*) Come here . . . last chance . . . no one makes a fool of me.

Mary Get back. No one's making a fool of you—you are a fool. Go and play games somewhere else.

Shadrach gets hold of her with his left hand and raises the knife in his right. John and Thomas leap to their feet

Jesus (*rising quietly*) Put that down . . . the rest of you—sit down.

Shadrach (*lifts the knife higher, sways on his feet, looks as though he might hit Jesus with it*) . . . no orders from you . . . teach respect for personal property . . . Kill you!

Jesus Put it down! Better still—give it to me.

Shadrach See both of us in grave first—presumptuous . . . peasant . . . (*All this time Jesus fixes him with a steady but profound stare—the whole company mesmerized into silence. Shadrach slowly lets it fall behind him where it quivers into the floor. Shadrach looks round, blusters, grabs Miriam*) Doesn't matter . . . all the same at night . . . can't see in the dark . . . go and find the horse . . . big, white, beautiful horse.

Salome It's black.

Shadrach Good . . . black all round . . . where's the horse?

Salome In Joseph's stables.

Shadrach . . . go and see it, now.

Shadrach totters out, Miriam giggling within his arm. Joseph looks thoughtfully at Jesus and at Mary, then he, too, rises

Joseph Come, Salome, we'll all go.

Salome takes Joseph's arm, Jacob gets up, puts his arm round her other side, they all go out, whispering and laughing

Mary (*defiant but dignified*) I suppose I ought to apologize for my friends.

Thomas Nasty moment that, nasty fellow too. (*Laughs*) Bet he'll keep a civil tongue in his head next time he meets you.

Mary He's usually very well-mannered. At this stage they get coarse and noisy. (*As an afterthought*) That's why I don't drink.

John Good heavens, don't you drink wine?

Mary (*shakes her head*) Water, milk, that's all. Don't look so surprised. We all have our personal dimensions of morality. I can't bear to lose control of myself. I like to know exactly what I'm doing.

Thomas Doesn't sound very cosy . . . you're a strange girl . . . isn't she a strange girl?

Jesus I know she's very beautiful, very intelligent, but I don't know anything else about her . . . yet.

Mary for some reason has been robbed of her usual cool poise. She gets up and flits about, picks up the lyre and strums on it, almost as though she wanted the attention to pass from her

Tell me, do you like these parties?

Mary I was waiting for that.

Jesus Yes?

Mary That sort of question . . . variations on the same old theme; you know, what's a nice girl like you doing in a place like this?

Jesus Well?

Mary What else is there to do? Women in this country have such a dull time. I get so bored. I want to go to Rome.

Thomas They wouldn't know what hit them!

Jesus Why don't you go?

Mary Well, I'd have to tie myself down, wouldn't I? I mean I'd have to go with one particular man. It would be a bit limiting, wouldn't it?

Thomas I've never heard a woman talking like you.

Mary Well, I never felt any inclination to be faithful to one man; it seems a fool's game to me.

John Oughtn't we to be going? The others will wonder what happened to us.

Jesus There's no hurry. We'll go soon.

Mary No—don't go, please don't go! (*Jesus looks steadily at her. She rushes into explanations*) It's just that we've only just met. I may never see you again.

Jesus (*after a pause*) That's up to you.

Mary (*another pause*) Does that mean—I may see you again?

Jesus (*abruptly*) I saw your father the other day. Do you know that he misses you?

Mary (*astounded*) You know my father?

Jesus (*smiling*) I know all your family, Simon—I like your father—Martha who amuses me very much, and Lazarus . . . I like to think Lazarus is one of my closest friends.

Mary Fancy that! Well, let me tell you, none of them miss me, none of them. Martha, whom you find so amusing, hates me; I can never do anything right for her. She brought me up, but I know she found me a burden to her.

Jesus They told me that when your father was very ill for so long you nursed him with the utmost devotion and wouldn't let anyone else run the risk of being near him.

Mary He's better now. He doesn't need me.

Thomas What was wrong with him?

Mary Don't tell him.

Jesus Why not? He was a leper. (*Everyone looks very shocked*)

Judas You nursed him through *that*?

Mary What would you expect me to do? Leper or no leper he was my father, wasn't he? Martha was scared to death.

Judas What happened? You said he was better. Lepers don't get better.

Mary He did. It cleared up all at once. None of us could believe it. I'd gone somewhere that afternoon; when I came home Martha was raving about some friend of Lazarus, some young man . . . who . . . called . . . (*Realization slowly dawns and she is suddenly afraid—whispering*) You! . . . it was you!

Pause

John Yes, it was him. I remember it now because he put his arms round your father, right round him, and your sister screamed and said "You mustn't embrace a leper", but he's better, isn't he?

Mary Yes . . . I don't know what I can say to you . . . what is there to say? He means a great deal to me.

Jesus He doesn't think that. He thinks you've forgotten him.

Mary (*violently*) I told you. He doesn't need me . . . and Martha doesn't want me home whatever she may have told you . . . anyway, I like to be amused . . . I like change, I like money . . . I like everything it buys. I'm not ashamed of myself. I like my life.

Jesus If you didn't it would all be a waste of time.

Mary Yes, and I like men! You might as well know the worst about me. I like lots of men. I get so bored. I can't settle. A husband and half a dozen kids would drive me mad.

Jesus There are other ways of curing boredom.

Mary Not for a woman.

Jesus (*emphatically*) Yes!

Mary What, for instance?

Jesus Sharing other people's lives. Identifying with them in sadness and pleasure. It's selfish people who are bored.

Mary (*like a small, rude child*) It sounds dull, very dull. Good people are always dull especially good women. And anyway, nobody likes nosy-parkers.

Jesus Other people's emotions and thoughts aren't dull, no exploration is ever dull.

Mary Nosy-parkers!

Thomas We're not nosy-parkers. We don't go where we're not wanted and we only give help where we're asked.

Judas finds all this strange but interesting

Jesus (*taking Mary's hand*) Listen! To search the unsearchable, to discover things hidden since the world began, is that dull? To walk on the frontiers of infinity, to reach out beyond, to see into the mind of God, is that dull? To love the unlovable, to bind up the broken hearts of the world, to find divinity in humanity, and where you don't find it to invoke it, is that dull? Have you ever seen God's eyes looking out of a man?

Mary No.

Jesus I have. Come, John, Thomas, you're right. It's late. We must go. Can you walk, Thomas?

Thomas Of course I can walk. I didn't have all that much.

Mary (*losing all her poise*) Don't go! Please don't go.

Jesus We have to go.

Mary Will I ever see you again?

Jesus (*pause*) What do you want me to say to you?

Mary (*urgently*) Don't you belong to some sort of community? I mean, you don't live at home, do you?

Jesus Sometimes we do. Not always.

Thomas If he stays away too long his mother's been known to come looking for him!

Jesus (*smiling*) As to a community, it's not really that. We have a few close friends. We go about together. When we run out of money we go back to our trades for a while.

Judas What do you do with your money?

John Give it away mostly. It's surprising how many people live in poverty in this great and glorious Roman Empire.

Mary (*an awful thought has slowly dawned on her*) It sounds a thoroughly unhealthy set-up to me. You all live together. You love each other. You share everything . . . My God! You're a bunch of queers!

Jesus, John, and Thomas are momentarily surprised, then they roar with laughter and exchange delighted looks

Jesus No indeed! We're all quite healthy, quite normal . . . I promise you! You'd have no doubt about that if they saw you. (*All the men laugh again*)

Mary (*still suspicious*) Have you no women with you?

Thomas No. And we don't want any. Damned nuisances. Trouble-makers.

Mary Who looks after you?

Jesus (*amused*) As you've heard, we have mothers. I find mine rather difficult to shake off sometimes. Some of us have wives.

Mary (*this is a new and unwelcome idea*) Have you a wife?

Thomas snorts

Jesus No.

Mary Then I'm coming with you. I won't be a nuisance, but I've got to come with you.

Thomas Got to?

Mary Well then—I *want* to come with you. At least, I don't want to come with *you*, but I want to be with *him*.

Jesus Do you? Why?

Mary I don't know why. (*Jesus looks at her steadily*) Well—yes, I do, but this is difficult for me. It's a new situation. I'm so used to men falling over themselves for me. Don't misunderstand me. I don't want that, but . . . I don't want to let you out of my sight . . . I want to be with you . . . don't say no!

There is a silence, everyone waits breathlessly

Jesus Get your cloak.

Mary goes out

Judas comes quickly over to Jesus

Judas (*earnestly*) You can't take her. Take me!
Jesus (*amused*) She'll be perfectly all right with us. We'll take good care of her.
Judas I'm not thinking of her. I'm thinking of you and the good name of your organization.
Jesus What organization? I have no organization. Don't worry. She'll be safe with us.
Judas Don't do this! When it gets round, you'll be the laughing-stock of Judea.
Jesus She needs us. What other people say or even think isn't important.
Judas (*quite irritated*) I don't even know you. I have no excuse for being persistent, but you're so—outrageously self-confident. Don't you ever have self-doubts?
Jesus About the way I do things—often; about what I have to do—never.
Judas (*gloomily*) Since the first moment I saw you I knew that your life and mine are somehow linked; not, I think, happily.
Jesus Yes . . . you realized that very quickly.
Judas I have to come with you.
Jesus (*hesitant*) I don't know . . .
Judas (*agitated*) Why? In heaven's name, why don't you know? You accept the girl knowing what she is and you hesitate about accepting me!
Jesus (*he pauses*) That girl has no reservations about me.
Judas So?
Jesus You have a great many, and always will have.
Thomas With all due respect you've led a soft life. We live rough.
Jesus Yes, indeed. That too. The foxes have holes and the birds of the air have nests, but often we have nowhere to lay our heads.
Judas I'm not soft. I can take anything you can. Let me come!
Jesus Why?
Judas I suppose I feel like the girl. When you talk, my own life seems flat, stale, and I can see the boundaries of the world pushed back, areas of experience I'd never dreamt of. I have to come.
Jesus So be it! Well, as you've probably gathered—this is Thomas! This is John! (*He puts an arm round each disciple*)
John You're a Judean, aren't you?
Judas Yes, but I'll do my best to fit in. I'll learn your ways.

John (*laughing*) There aren't any ways. No rules. Everybody's friendly. They'll welcome you.

Thomas Still, you'll be a bit of a novelty; we're all from Galilee.

John But they're a grand lot.

Jesus I hope you know what you're doing.

Judas I'm fed up—world-weary, you might say—no illusions, no hope either. I won't let you down.

John We don't even know your name.

Thomas No. What's your name, mate?

Judas Judas. Judas Iscariot.

BLACK-OUT

SCENE 2

A fortnight later

The house of Simon Peter's mother-in-law in Capernaum. Mary, mother of Jesus, and some of the disciples are staying there. A violent storm is in progress, thunder, lightning, wind, etc. Judas, Thomas, Mary, mother of Jesus, are in the room; the first two are agitated. Mary is mending something

Mary and Thomas sit, Judas prowls about

Judas I wish they were back.

Thomas They'll be all right.

There is a peal of thunder

Judas I don't like storms. It's childish, I know. I always feel like getting under the table.

Thomas There are a lot of people like that. It's nothing to be ashamed of.

Another peal

Judas Are you sure they'll be all right? The last time we had a storm like this two ships were lost, remember?

Thomas They asked for it. It was stormy when they went out.

Mary Don't worry, Judas. Peter knows the lake like his own kitchen. No storm ever frightened him. They'll be back.

The storm increases in fury. Judas paces about anxiously. Even Thomas gets up and looks out towards the lake

Judas Shall I go back to the beach?

Mary No, my dear. You've been once and you can't do anything—except get thoroughly wet again.

There is a blinding flash and a mighty roar of thunder, and then, dead silence. Thomas and Judas look startled, Mary unperturbed

Judas That ended quickly.

Mary Yes. It's the contrast, isn't it? It's so quiet.

Thomas It happens like that on the lake sometimes. One minute all hell's
let loose and the next—sunshine. Still—that did seem a bit sudden.
Judas I hope the boat stood up to it. The damage could have been done
already.
Mary (*with complete confidence*) They've got Jesus with them.
Judas Well, with all due respect, he's not a sailor, is he?
Mary He handles a boat very well.
Thomas But that isn't what she meant . . .
Judas No? What then?
Thomas Things have a way of working out when he's around.
Judas (*laughing*) You make him sound like some sort of magic talisman.
Mary You haven't been with him very long, have you?
Judas No.

Mary looks into the night

Mary They're here.
Judas Thank God!

> *Peter, John and Jesus enter. The first two look absolutely exhausted. Jesus
> looks, if anything, rather pleased with himself, as though he's enjoyed the
> outing. Peter and John sink on to benches*

Peter Don't say anything! I feel sick; just leave me alone a minute.
John He swallowed half the lake. So did I if it comes to that.
Jesus (*cheerfully*) Some storm! (*To Mary*) Were you worried?
Judas We thought we'd seen the last of you.
Mary You did. I didn't. I always know when there's anything wrong. This
time I wasn't worried. (*Jesus puts his arm round her shoulders and hugs her*)
Jesus We were lucky. May I have a towel?
Mary Yes, come on . . . I'll find you all dry clothes.

Jesus and Mary exit

Thomas He seems very cheerful. He must like these ordeals. I'll swear he
thrives on them.

*Peter and John look at each other. John has flung himself along the bench,
arms outstretched, both of them still puffing and panting*

John (*to Peter*) I don't believe it . . . it didn't happen.
Peter No. We imagined it.
John No, we didn't. I've never been so frightened in my life. I didn't
imagine *that*.
Peter Any other man . . . I'd say he was mad.
John He can't be mad . . . because it works.
Peter Uncanny! Never saw anything like it.
Judas Thomas said you were never frightened of storms.
Peter (*indignant*) Of course I'm not frightened of storms. Who the devil
said I was?

John Who's talking about storms?

Thomas You are, aren't you? Did the wind blow out your wits?

Peter (*still indignant*) I'm not frightened of storms.

Judas Of what, then?

Peter (*reluctantly*) Him!

Thomas (*interested*) He's talking about Jesus.

Judas You were frightened of Jesus? Not of Jesus!

John It's not a blind bit of good you being superior . . . *we* . . . *were* . . .
frightened!

Judas You must be joking! Not of Jesus!

Peter Could *you* have slept through that? That was the first thing . . .
He went on sleeping!

Thomas He was tired.

John I thought he was dead!

Judas Well, what happened then?

John You tell them.

Peter Nothing. We woke him and he stood up.

Judas What frightened you?

Peter He kept laughing.

Judas Laughing?

Thomas You'll learn. He's got a funny sense of humour.

John Peter's right. It was uncanny. He was laughing, exulting in the storm,
laughing *with* it.

Peter Just stood there drenched with rain, his face lifted up, lightning,
thunder, all round . . . Laughing!

Judas Laughing—*with* the wind?

Peter That's right, as though it was a friend or something—it was
crazy.

Thomas I think the world of him, you know, but sometimes I wonder if he's
quite right in the head.

Judas How did it all end?

John Quite suddenly, he stopped laughing and shouted over the storm and
it stopped.

Judas Just like that?

John Just like that.

Judas Coincidence.

John Yes, of course.

Judas So why were you frightened?

Peter He *told* it to stop.

Thomas (*laughing*) What? Come off it!

Peter Well, he shouted—right over the storm—and that was it!

Judas (*sarcastic*) Like taming a wild animal?

John Exactly like that.

Judas Oh, come now, you're talking to *me*, not to one of your Galilean
peasants!

Peter Bloody cheek!

Mary re-enters

Mary Come on, you lads, who's going to coddle you when you've got colds? I've enough work to do. (*Looks from one face to another*) What's going on here?

Judas (*still sarcastic*) These gentlemen, ma'am, are suggesting that your son stopped the storm! Did you suspect he was responsible for weather conditions on the sea of Galilee?

Mary (*quite calm*) I shouldn't wonder.

Judas (*astonished*) With due respect, is everybody mad around here or have I walked into a fairy tale?

Mary (*still quite unruffled*) Perhaps.

Jesus re-enters, rubbing his hair with a towel

Jesus Mary's putting your soup out. I've had mine; and Peter—your wife wants you . . . you'd better hurry up.

Peter, Thomas and John go out. Mary follows more slowly. Judas makes no move to go and after a glance at him Jesus, too, sits. Then he hands Judas the towel

Jesus Your hair's wet. Where've you been? Did you go out?

Judas (*absent-minded*) Yes. On the beach. (*Giving his hair a rub*) I was worried.

Jesus About us?

Judas You know very well. About *you*. (*Pause*) Why did you do it?

Jesus Do what?

Judas (*slow and deliberate*) Let them think that you were responsible for what happened out there? (*Jesus is silent and gazes in front of him*) What did you say to them?

Jesus (*quietly*) Nothing much. I was asleep when it started. When I woke up they were in a panic. I told them not to be frightened.

Judas And they ended up more frightened than they were before. (*Pause*) There must be more to it than this. What did you *do*?

Jesus Tell me, Judas. Are you happy here with us?

Judas With *you*—yes. You haven't answered my question.

Jesus What did I do?

Judas Yes.

Jesus Is it so important to you? You weren't there.

Judas Yes. Because whatever it was, you misled them somehow. You ought to *know* this. They think you've got supernatural powers. I want to hear your version. What happened out there?

Jesus You sound like a prosecuting counsel.

Judas Why won't you give me a straight answer?

Jesus Because I don't think you're quite ready for this sort of conversation.

Judas (*shouting*) For God's sake don't act the fool with me. What did you *do*?

Jesus It was a bad storm. Worse than usual. I thought the boat would turn over.

Judas Well?

Jesus (*smiling*) I willed it to go away.

Judas (*furious at being made a fool of*) This is a joke.

Jesus (*suddenly serious*) No.

Judas How can that be possible?

Jesus (*smiling*) Prayer. Through it you tap the source of all power, which is God.

Judas Prayer?

Jesus Prayer is *power*.

Judas Power?

Jesus Of course. Power over yourself first, power over others indirectly, and power over things. Look! You see that rock over there? If you believed it, really believed it, you could move that by sheer will-power, and hurl it into the sea.

Judas It doesn't make sense.

Jesus No. That's why you couldn't do it—it doesn't make sense, your sort of sense. But some of them could, some of them will when they find out their own strength. Some of them will do greater things than that.

Judas You're asking me to accept things that are outside nature, beyond reason.

Jesus How do you know they're outside nature and beyond reason? There is no area of activity *beyond* God. Everything is contained within him. In his name, there is no limit and never will be to a man's scope.

Judas God gave me reason, and my reason tells me that these things are impossible. My reason says man can't control nature and disease. These are tricks to deceive the eye.

Jesus If your reason tells you that, Judas, then the horizons of your thinking are too narrow. You are limiting God.

Judas On the contrary, it is God who has limited *me*. How can he limit me and then ask me to accept things beyond those limits?

Jesus He has *not* limited you . . . You have imagination, faith, inspiration, instincts, as well as your reason; as much a part of you as your reason. When you deny these things in yourself, you limit the power of God in you. You give him too small a field to work in. You reduce him to your dimensions. (*Laughing*) You say "Because *my* little brain can't grasp this, it can't be true! I, Judas, scholar at the feet of Gamaliel, have passed judgement on the kingdom of the Almighty! This I cannot understand—it is too big for my reason to apprehend—therefore I dismiss it—it cannot be true!" This is intellectual arrogance!

Judas (*angry*) It's you who are intellectually arrogant! At your age how can you profess to be so wise? These are words you're twisting to suit your own theories. Who do you think you are? God's fresh air, blowing through the mists of the world?

Jesus (*smiling*) That's a very good definition.

Judas (*still angry*) It's impossible to argue with you. You've got an unfair way of taking the wind out of one's sails. Your sincerity convinces me, your words don't. And I don't know how to reason with you. I'm just not credulous like the others.

Jesus (*also angry*) Don't underestimate them. Formal education doesn't necessarily turn a fool into a wise man. It only makes him knowledgeable. Sometimes knowledge is the greatest barrier to truth.

Judas There you go again! Clever talk, and what does it all mean? It just sounds good.

Jesus (*suddenly quiet*) If that's all it is to you, I wonder that you stay. There's no compulsion. You wanted to come . . .

Judas Yes—I—did—more than I ever wanted anything . . . I thought it would be different . . . I thought I would be your friend. You don't need me . . . I don't think you need friends . . .

Jesus My God! I don't think there was ever a more false conclusion.

Mary, his mother, calls from off stage—"Jesus! Jesus!" She comes in very agitated

Jesus We're coming. What is it?

Judas (*tense*) I'm sorry. (*Jesus puts his hand on his shoulder*)

Mary Will you hurry? It's Peter's mother-in-law; she's been taken ill.

Jesus What happened? An accident?

Mary She just collapsed. I hope it isn't a stroke. Her breathing's funny.

Judas (*very anxious to atone*) Shall I go for a doctor? Shall I send to Jerusalem?

Jesus I'll go. Where is she?

Mary They put her in her own bed.

Jesus goes hurriedly out

Judas We must have a doctor. I'll pay. We must spare no expense.

Mary (*kindly*) You are very thoughtful. It won't be necessary, my dear.

Judas But she may die!

Mary No, she won't die. She's got Jesus with her.

Mary exits.
Judas is left alone, troubled

BLACK-OUT

A young man strolls on to the front of the stage; spotlight follows him. He comes right to the audience, sits informally on the apron with a very confidential manner. He is Thomas, and he is the Narrator. He could walk right out on a catwalk into the audience

(*Wherever the Narrator appears, during the previous black-out the scene including the actors is set and the players form a tableau which comes to life as the Narrator joins them*)

Thomas Those three years we spent together were wonderful, unforgettable, often tiring, often heart-breaking, but always exciting. What I remember most is the crowds. There was no rest for any of us, especially him, no rest, no peace; they followed him in droves. There always seemed to be hundreds of them, from first thing in the morning till last thing at night and some of them would wait all night and many nights to see him. Waiting—wanting—always wanting—I shall see them all my life, hands lifted in supplication—wanting—all wanting something of him. But they were happy years. We seemed to do a lot of laughing in those days. Sometimes people would come up to us hoping to take the micky out of him, you know the sort, snobs, smart alecs, so-called intellectuals. It never came off. They were the ones who ended up looking silly and we'd all roar with laughter. Yes, they were great days . . . (*Very chatty*) Of course, my name's Thomas, you know that. I'm what's known as a sceptic. If I say a thing happened, you can take it from me that it happened. I don't convince easily; I have to see things with my own eyes. I told Jesus this from the beginning. I said, "I'm not a gullible fool, you know; I won't believe anything just because someone else tells me it is so. It has to be in black and white for me. It has to make sense." Now, he seemed to find that funny; mind you, he's got a queer sense of humour. He said, "That's fair, Thomas; we'll play it by ear." Not that I was any worse than the others. I doubt if any of them really understood him except John, and in the beginning, I used to think Judas. For a while he and Judas were very close. They were alike in a way, both very quick-witted, both very clever. They'd have conversations and the rest of us were way behind. Then things began to go wrong between them. Judas got miserable about something and was always finding fault. Looking back, I suppose it really came to a head that day in Bethany . . .

The spot fades from him. He walks away. The stage lights go up on . . .

SCENE 3

Three years later.

The house of Simon, once known as Simon the leper, in Bethany. Martha and Mary are clearing away the remnants of a meal and go out almost at once. John is mending a sandal, Peter and Thomas are repairing a large fishing-net between them.

Thomas I think he's up to something. That's twice he's gone to Jerusalem this week.

John He goes to see his relatives, I suppose.

Peter I thought he didn't bother with them any more. He told me they didn't want to know him.

Thomas He's up to something . . .

Judas comes in

Talk of the devil! Where've you been? The Master was asking for you.

Peter You didn't say you'd be gone this long.

Judas (*slightly caustic*) Aren't we free to come and go as we like any more?
John Of course we are. What's the matter with you?
Judas It's not me, it's you, all of you. Something queer's going on . . .
the Master wants this . . . the Master wants that . . . what does the
Master say? A few months ago he was just Jesus. I liked it better then.
Peter Well, call him Jesus! We don't have to call him Master. He didn't
say so.
Judas Why do you, then?
Peter I don't know, it seems right.
Judas We're all equal in this community.
John Of course we're all equal. Why get so angry?
Judas I don't like some of the things he says. He gets a bit above himself.
Peter (*gets up*) I'll bloody thump you if you say another word—he's
worth two of you any day.
John Shut up, Peter. I want to know what he's on about. Shut up and sit
down.
Peter (*sits down muttering*) Bloody southerner!
John Now then—what do you mean—"gets above himself"?
Judas (*a bit sheepish but defiant*) I can give you plenty of examples. Last
night he said, "If you love me do as I say!"
John Well?
Judas Well!! I ask you, what friend talks to other friends like that? It's
imposing an intolerable burden on friendship. It puts obligations on
love where there should be none.
John I don't think you've got hold of the right end of the stick.

Martha bustles in with some dishes

Martha Where've you been all this time?
Judas Don't you start.
Martha Do you want food?
Judas No, thank you. I've eaten. (*Prowling about*) Anyway, it's not just
me. The temper of the crowd's changed lately, too.
John I can't say I've noticed it.
Peter Nor me. They're as thick as ever.
Judas That incident last week could have been very nasty.
Martha (*standing still in concern*) What was that?
Judas The crowd turned on him. They picked up stones.
Martha You didn't tell us.
John It was all right. He handled it.
Thomas Still—it could have been nasty.
Peter It wouldn't have got that far. I'd have sorted them out, only he
wouldn't let me.
John Anyway, it wasn't the usual type of crowd.
Judas What does that mean?
John Hoodlums, planted there deliberately. They were well paid, too.
Judas How do you know?
John Jesus told me. He found out.

Martha goes out

Judas Why does he tell you everything? It's a real closed shop, isn't it? You and Peter, John. The rest of us might as well go home!

John gets up, puts his arm round him affectionately

John Don't talk rubbish. What would we do without you?

Judas laughs and thumps him on the back. By nature he is a very nice young man, but he has a great anxiety complex about everything. He now walks round sniffing the air. John fetches a tool from a box and sits down again at his sandal. One after the other they look up at Judas, look at each other, shrug, etc.

Thomas What are you doing that for?

Judas What?

Thomas Sniffing about like a hungry dog. Martha offered you food.

Judas There's a queer smell!

Thomas It's Peter's feet.

Peter It's not! I washed them this morning!

Thomas Well, it's your sandal, then, that John's mending. I'm sure it is, because Peter's feet have a very distinctive smell.

Judas No. This is a pleasant smell. It doesn't smell of Peter!

John It's the supper.

Judas No, it isn't; it's different from cooking.

John I know what it is!

Thomas What?

John The spikenard.

Judas What?

John It's a kind of perfume, very heavy and rich.

Judas *(impatient)* Yes, I know what it is. What's it doing here?

Thomas Yes, that's what it is. I can smell it now. *(General agreement, but no one says any more. Judas is curious and good-humoured.)*

Judas What did I miss? No, don't tell me! The Governor's wife came to supper!

Thomas I wouldn't mind at that. She's a real dishy piece!

John I've heard she's a very nice woman, too.

Peter It's the oil they use to anoint the kings. I thought you knew everything.

Judas Are we celebrating the Passover in Jerusalem this year?

Peter Yes, we've taken a room at an inn in the lower town.

Judas Well, I'll tell you now, we'd be better off going back to Galilee. The atmosphere's dangerous in Jerusalem.

Thomas You did go to Jerusalem, then?

Judas So? Where are the kings?

John This conversation gets more and more involved, everybody's at cross-purposes. What kings?

Judas The kings you were talking about with the perfume.

Thomas Oh, that! There were no kings, fathead! Mary poured it over

Jesus at supper. As a matter of fact, she got morbid and cried all over him.

John It was upsetting.

Judas (*very wary and himself upset*) She did what?

John She poured this oil on him.

Judas Jesus has not expressed any wish to be treated as royalty, has he?

John No, of course not. Don't start getting emotional about it.

Judas Then why did she do it?

Thomas Who can say? Who understands Mary?

Judas (*persistent*) Had they arranged it between them?

John Don't be daft! It was a gesture. A bit hysterical perhaps, but harmless.

Thomas It was embarassing. I felt rather awkward.

John We all did. It was so unexpected.

Judas Think carefully. Are you positive he didn't know about it?

John Of course we are.

Thomas He was as surprised as we were.

Peter It certainly shook him. He went very quiet afterwards.

Judas Why did she do it?

John Oh, for heaven's sake! It was simply to show how much she cares for him. It was the most expensive thing she'd got to give.

Judas Where did she get it from?

Peter I don't suppose it was all that expensive.

Thomas Yes, it was. Martha told me a single ounce costs pounds, *very* expensive.

Judas How did she come to have it?

Thomas That's easily explained. It was a relic of her dancing days. Somebody gave it to her.

Judas (*very sarcastic*) That's a questionable source for a royal anointing.

Peter (*tactlessly*) That hadn't struck me. You'd think she'd want to forget that part of her life.

Judas (*very cold*) You would think so, wouldn't you? (*He gnaws at the subject like a bone*) I want to know why she did it. There *must* have been a reason. He *must* have said something to put the idea into her head.

Thomas For God's sake, shut up! Is it so very important?

Judas (*pause*) It might be—yes, indeed, it might well be.

John Stop going on and on about it. You're so damned cautious anyway, you wouldn't understand in a thousand years.

Judas (*shouting*) I'm the only one around here who's using his head. You'll be sorry you didn't listen to me.

Martha enters

Martha What on earth's going on? What's the matter with you all? You never used to bicker like this. If you're going to brawl, out you go till you've cooled off!

Judas (*contrite*) Sorry, Martha. It was my fault. It's just that it seems such nonsense . . .

At this point, Jesus comes in unseen by Judas and stands still

Martha What does?

Judas Well, Jesus is always so very concerned about the poor and it could have been sold for a lot of money and we could have given it away. It seems wasteful, to say the least, to use it for some demonstration Jesus didn't even want.

As Judas finishes speaking, Jesus moves down to him

Jesus (*expressionlessly*) The poor will always be with you.

Judas looks uncomfortable, the others anxious

How were things in Jerusalem?

Judas (*abruptly, still upset*) Bad! Everybody—Herodians, Pharisees, Sadducees, the Establishment all after our blood.

Jesus What are they complaining about?

Judas (*bitterly*) Oh, it's neatly tabulated—witchcraft, heresy, insurrection. They say that everything you've done has been with the help of the devil.

Jesus Fools! Typical of the way they distort truth to suit themselves. Would the Prince of devils cast out his own subordinates? (*They all laugh, but not Judas*)

Judas That's not the worst of it.

Jesus No? What then?

Judas You're treading on sacred ground, hence dangerous ground.

Jesus says nothing, looks at him and waits

Well—it's true, isn't it? You say things that offend tradition. They say you make outrageous claims.

Jesus Such as?

Judas You're supposed to have said that you're the Son of God.

Jesus (*laughs*) You're *all* Sons of God, though I must say sometimes I find it hard to believe. (*He takes some figs off table, unconcerned—Judas grabs his wrist*)

Judas You can be stoned if they can prove that you've uttered a blasphemy.

Jesus (*rather dryly. Taking his hand away*) I'm as well versed in the law as you, my friend. My regard for it is as high. Perhaps the difference is that I'm more concerned for its spirit than its letter. (*He sits down by Peter. He picks up a portion of net*) We'll have to go fishing again soon.

Thomas Yes, we will. Judas says we're running short of money.

Judas inclines his head

Jesus (*laughing*) Never mind, we'll send him to borrow some from his uncle, Caiaphas.

Judas (*injured*) He's only my uncle about three times removed. Anyway, can I help it if I'm related to the high priest's family. I don't even like him. I don't like any of them.

Jesus That's what comes of mixing with low company the past three years. You've lost your taste for elegant living. (*They all laugh at Judas*)

Judas (*accusingly, to Jesus*) You laugh at all the wrong things. I wish
   you'd be serious at a time like this. (*Jesus looks at him, Judas looks sulky*)
   You and I don't seem to understand each other any more.

Jesus (*suddenly serious*) Was there a time when we did?

Judas I thought so.

Jesus Sometimes I think you'd have been happier with that community of
   Essenes on the Dead Sea shore there. World-negation, life-negation,
   austerity, fasting, that's more in your line.

Thomas (*resigned*) Here they go again . . .

Judas That's not true . . .

John How do you know so much about them?

Jesus I stayed with them once, for a month or two.

Peter What for?

Jesus I thought they might have had some answers . . .

John And did they?

Jesus No. At least, not for me.

Judas (*blurting this out*) There's nowhere I'd rather be than with you.

Jesus I know that.

Judas It's just that—well, you don't seem to realize what you're walking into.

Jesus (*rises from floor*) Judas, I know only too well what I'm walking into.
   Have you lost faith in me altogether?

Judas You're rushing into disaster.

Jesus In this life, disasters are inevitable, but the man who precipitates
   them needlessly is a fool.

Judas (*not listening*) There was this business of Mary tonight.

Jesus Yes . . . I was wondering when we'd get round to that.

Judas It was an *extraordinary* thing to do, absolutely uncalled for, and so
   open to misinterpretation . . . (*Jesus looks at him quite impassive and
   Judas rushes on*) The same with that gesture the other day, riding into
   Jerusalem like a conquering hero, and when someone asked you why you
   let them give you a king's greeting, you said, "Why not?"

Jesus (*laughing*) Well—why not?

Judas But it's such a peculiar answer, you're laying yourself open to misinterpretation.

Jesus By whom? (*No reply*) By you, Judas?

Judas Well, yes, if you like. By me and others. (*Miserably*) I want us all
   to go back to Galilee. (*Childishly*) I want to go fishing.

Jesus (*rising wearily*) It's too late to run away. Things have gone too far.
   Make up your mind, Judas. He that is not for me is against me.

Martha comes in looking agitated

Martha There's a woman at the door with a young girl. She looks a bit of
   an idiot to me; she just gawps and says nothing. They want to see you.

Peter Oh no! Send them away. It's been a long day. We're all tired.

Thomas Tell them to come back tomorrow.

Jesus Send her in, Martha.

Martha There's just one thing . . .

Jesus Yes?
Martha Well—she's not one of us.
Jesus What on earth do you mean? She's a woman, isn't she?
Martha Yes, but she's a Samaritan.
Thomas That settles it, then. Send her packing. Cheeky monkeys!
Jesus Send her in, Martha. (*He looks round the disciples one at a time and one by one they look guilty and uneasy*)

Two women come in, one middle-aged, quite prosperous-looking, and the other young, frightened

Good evening.

None of the disciples look very enthusiastic

Judas (*politely*) Won't you sit down?

Both women sit

John You're a long way from home.
Judas Need knows no frontiers.

She looks gratefully at him, and he and Jesus exchange a look

Jesus What can I do for you?
Woman I know some of you don't feel very well disposed towards us, but if you can't help there's no help anywhere.
Jesus How can you be so sure? You've never seen me before.
Woman No. But I've heard things . . .
Jesus Is it the girl? (*Woman nods*) Come here! (*Girl comes to him slowly; he puts his hands on her shoulders and looks into her eyes*) Are you ill?

She shakes her head

She can hear, but she can't speak. How long has she been like this?
Thomas From birth, I should think.
Jesus No. It's recent. Am I right?
Woman Yes, sir.
Jesus How long?
Woman Five years. Her parents were killed . . . it was the main street in Samaria . . . young Roman officers racing chariots . . . just acting the fool. She saw it happen—ever since she's been like this. I've seen doctors, priests. Nobody can do anything.
Jesus And you are?
Woman Her aunt. Her mother's sister.
Jesus You love her very much?
Woman Why else would I bring her to you?
Jesus Why is it so important that she talk? She has her other faculties.
Woman But she's a young girl, isn't she? I want her to enjoy life fully, to know what it is to have friendship and love. I want her to talk to *me*. My husband is dead, I have no child of my own. I think of her as a daughter and I want her to have everything.

The girl looks distressed and holds her hands out to her

Jesus (*to the girl*) And you? Do you feel she's been a mother to you? Do you want to please her? (*Girl nods*) Do you want to *talk* to her? (*The girl nods her head*) Well, you see how it is. The wheel has come full circle for you two. When your mother died you needed her, but now *she* needs *you* . . . She has no one else . . . Do you love her? (*The girl nods again—upset*) Then there is no reason why you can't speak, every reason why you should. Do you trust me? (*Nods again*) Very well, then you *can* speak and you will . . . What is your name?

There is a long, breathless pause

Girl (*slowly but distinctly*) Ruth . . . sir.
Jesus Good. That is a pretty name. Do you know the story of Ruth and Naomi?
Girl Yes, sir. (*Suddenly she realizes she is talking easily. She jumps with delight, claps her hands, hugs her aunt. All in the room including Jesus smile with her*)
Woman I can't thank you . . . what they said about you is true. Is there anything I can do for you? Anything?
Jesus (*smiling—breaking tension*) Yes. Go with Martha and have something to eat before you go home.
Woman My feet will have wings and the journey will seem short; we shall have so much to say!
Girl Thank you, sir. (*Suddenly she kneels to him, kisses his hands, bursts into tears*)

Martha and her aunt take her out

John You were right to see them.
Peter We get used to you. It's being with you all the time. We forget how you seem to other people, as it was with us . . . three years ago.
Jesus (*again laughing*) A prophet is always without honour in his own country! (*He yawns*) I'm tired. I think I'll go to bed. (*He turns to go*)
Judas Just a minute! Jesus!
Jesus Yes?
Judas (*tense*) Why do they all kneel to you?
Jesus (*expressionless*) Do I ask them to?
Judas No. But why do you let them?

Jesus looks at him, says nothing, goes out

Thomas (*savagely*) Why can't you leave him alone? You're always at him. He's got enough on his mind without you turning sour on him.

Goes out after Jesus

Judas (*head in hands, in despair and misery*) Things crowd in on us so fast and everything's going wrong . . .

John I don't understand you . . . how . . . wrong?

Judas Ever since that day at Caesarea Philippi . . . he said, "Who do you think I am?" as though we didn't know. What does he mean? What's he doing? What does he want? He's changed.

John Rubbish. Not one iota. It's you who's changed. If you'd been with us that time on the mountain you'd have stopped asking yourself silly questions.

Judas (*shouting with anger*) Yes—and why wasn't I with you? Because you three had gone off on your own as usual.

Peter (*ignoring him*) It was queer that—all that light! Something happened to him.

John Did it? I'm not so sure. I think we saw him for a few minutes as he really is.

Judas (*getting up abruptly and standing in triumph over John*) That's it! That's it! That's exactly what I'm talking about.

Peter Well, nobody else knows what you're talking about.

Judas Yes, they do and you do. You don't want to face up to it. Go on, say it! Put it into words . . . you daren't!

Peter Judas! For the love of God leave us in peace. Just leave us alone. I want to finish this net.

Judas (*ignoring him*) John knows, don't you? Come on John . . . *put it into words!*

John (*quite calmly*) There's no need to put it into words.

Judas (*violently*) I can't stand much more of this, this acceptance of the ridiculous. It's making me sick.

Peter and John stare at him silently. He goes out

Peter What's the matter with him? I thought he loved Jesus.

John Yes he does.

Peter Well then?

John I don't know. I don't know. But I feel very uneasy about it.

BLACK-OUT

SCENE 4

A few days later

This is the house of the High Priest Caiaphas. Annas, his father-in-law, the ex-High Priest, has not really abdicated his office. He is a waspish creature, full of himself, and always interfering

Caiaphas Well now, Father Annas, this begins to look more promising.

Annas (*he has an irritating habit of pursuing his own train of thought and not listening*) I gather the heckling party in the Temple didn't go any too well?

Caiaphas (*very cold because he organized it*) That was not my doing. However, the wonder boy of Nazareth has overplayed his hand.

Annas Have you cause to think so?

Caiaphas If the fact that Judas is outside waiting to unburden himself is anything to go by!

Annas (*very surprised, but not going to admit it. He pauses and sniffs*) About time he came to his senses and saw where his real duty lies. It's no credit to the family that he went off with that riff-raff in the first place. I would have thought you could have found him something useful to do.

Caiaphas (*dryly*) He doesn't like priests.

Annas Shocking crowd to associate with! Low tradesmen, labourers, tax collectors and worse, undesirable ragamuffins every one of them. What put him off them?

Caiaphas I'm not sure. I don't think he liked that foolish demonstration with the donkey. But one thing worries me.

Annas Well?

Caiaphas Judas is a very intelligent young man.

Annas He ought to be after all that education.

Caiaphas He's also honest.

Annas He'll grow out of that.

Caiaphas For a priest you're cynical beyond the point of decency, Father Annas. Now tell me this—what is there about this man Jesus that kept Judas by his side for three years?

Annas When we've answered that question, my son, we'll know how to deal with the situation.

Judas comes in looking miserable

Judas They told me to come in. Am I too early?

Annas No, indeed. Sit down, my boy. You look very tired.

Both Priests do their best to register sympathy. Judas is genuinely distressed and confused. In this scene he rouses pity and possibly irritation

Caiaphas You look ill. Are you ill?

Judas No, sir.

Caiaphas What then? Are you in trouble?

Judas Yes, sir, indeed I am.

Caiaphas What is it?

Judas May I speak freely?

Caiaphas Of course. What are families for?

Judas I misled you.

Annas Not intentionally, I'm sure.

Caiaphas How misled us?

Judas I'm so confused. I know that we have caused the authorities some concern. I told you it was needless. I answered to you for his absolute integrity.

Caiaphas Well?

Judas I'm not sure . . . I'm not sure. I need someone to talk to. I could be wrong.

Caiaphas You've known him a long time.

Judas I would have trusted him with my life.

Annas And now?

Judas He's either a hypocrite or insane . . . and if it's either one or the other, can we trust him?

Annas Oh dear, dear, dear!

Caiaphas Perhaps all this fuss has gone to his head? The applause of the crowd has knocked him off his balance?

Annas That's it. A touch of harmless vanity perhaps?

Judas No. It's worse than that. It's not vanity as you and I know it. It's more serious than that.

Caiaphas Try to give an example.

Judas It's not just isolated incidents. It's the accumulation of many impressions, an atmosphere created, homage out of all proportion given and accepted.

Annas An example would help.

Judas I hesitate to tell you. The other day there was this. He's always saying that God is his father, *his* father I think he means in a special sense, and Philip said to him, "Show us the Father and we won't ask anything else."

Annas (*tittering*) Gracious me! He didn't want much.

Judas No. I grant you that. The question was ridiculous. It's the sort of thing they say to him . . . You should have heard the answer . . .

Caiaphas Yes . . . go on!

Judas (*his voice drops in awe, disbelief, perplexity, as he says this*) He said, "Have I been such a long time with you, Philip, and you haven't known me?"

Annas and Caiaphas are profoundly shocked and they look at each other incredulously

Caiaphas This is serious.

Annas Megalomania.

Caiaphas Insanity—poor young man, let us be charitable.

Judas Yes—but this is where confusion comes in. You *can't* listen to him and live with him and think he's insane. It must be something else . . . Is it hypocrisy? Surely *he* can't believe in the implications of the things he says? Or is it pride? . . . It frightens me to be with him sometimes. He has this self-confidence, it's unbelievable, it's indescribable. He doesn't *need* anybody.

Annas (*piously*) Spiritual pride is a great sin.

Caiaphas For my part I feel sorrow. It grieves me that a young man who is obviously a cut above the usual run of carpenters should be so corrupted by an evil imagination and so misled by ideas of grandeur that he sets himself up as some Divine Authority.

Annas He'd have done better to stick to his trade.

Judas I don't know. He's done a great deal of good.

Annas What he doesn't know is this, that when the crowd tires of him, as they will, as they do of all novelties, they'll turn and rend him.

Judas That mustn't happen.

Caiaphas Well, you've told us your side of it. Now hear ours. Pilate has learnt that we're not to be trifled with. That doesn't mean we can push him too far. In the past ten days I have received two official complaints about this friend of yours. He attracts these huge crowds. He does far too much talking and his behaviour as a whole is highly questionable and suspicious. Has he political aspirations?

Judas (*uneasy*) I don't know. Sometimes I think so. I know the Zealots have been in touch with him.

Caiaphas Are you a Zealot, Judas?

Judas I was—not any more. I don't like their methods.

Annas This gets worse and worse. Is there anything else you can tell us? Think!

Judas There is something . . . but I may have misunderstood.

Caiaphas Let us be the judge of that.

Judas As we were coming down into Jerusalem he said there would come a day soon when not a stone of it would be left standing. I couldn't see how he could say that if he didn't know something.

Caiaphas The evidence seems to pile up. This is very disturbing.

Annas Is he coming into the city for the Passover?

Judas Yes. Every day. At night we go back to Bethany to stay with friends.

Caiaphas I see. Well, something must be done.

Annas Careful, my son, now! Careful! We don't want a riot with Pilate in residence.

Caiaphas I know. I've thought of that. Judas! I'm going to be quite honest with you. Obviously you're disturbed about your friend's motives and intentions or you wouldn't be here. Am I right?

Judas Yes, sir.

Caiaphas Very well, then. Do you agree that sooner or later I've got to come face to face with this Jesus and we must thrash out a few matters together?

Judas Yes, I suppose so.

Caiaphas There are many issues at stake here. Perhaps the greatest is the safety of all Israel. That includes the safety of every soul who lives here. This must be *my* primary consideration.

Judas What do you want me to do?

Caiaphas Let us know when we can find him unprotected by those hysterical crowds. We can then persuade him to come here quietly without causing a commotion. Obviously I've got to talk to him.

Judas There must be no question of harm coming to him.

Caiaphas We are not Roman barbarians.

Judas Very well, I'll do it. But he must be treated with every courtesy.

Caiaphas Naturally. We understand that.

Judas (*reaction sets in. He looks sick*) May I go now?

Caiaphas Of course. We are very grateful to you.

Annas (*clearing his throat*) There is a small matter . . . the Sanhedrin is in the habit of donating a small fee, a reward as you might say, for informing on the activities of anti-government elements. We would like you to have it.(*Offers a small purse to Judas*)

Judas (*horrified*) No! No indeed! I'm not an informer and Jesus is not a traitor. He may be misguided, that's a different matter.
Annas They tell me you are very kind to the poor. Take it and give it away.
Judas I couldn't take money!
Annas It's part of the regulations. Information has to be paid for.
Caiaphas Don't force it on him, Father Annas. We respect his delicacy.
Annas Very well then. We shall expect to hear from you.

Judas goes out looking, if anything, more disturbed than when he came in

(*Sniffs*) Very affecting!
Caiaphas Well, really. You surpassed yourself there.
Annas I have not the pleasure of understanding you.
Caiaphas Trying to pay him for betraying his friend! You nearly threw away any chance we have of apprehending him.
Annas You're not as clever as you think, my son. If we'd put it on a business basis, it would be the less easy for him to go back on his word.
Caiaphas He won't do that. (*Ruthless*) This Nazarene has got to be silenced. Mark my words, if he isn't, these streets will run with blood. Of course, Rome won't care two hoots about this talk of Divinity. They turn their own emperors into gods at the drop of a hat. It's way of keeping the population in order. Nobody takes it seriously.
Annas We get him on the charge of insurrection then?
Caiaphas Of course.
Annas And if we anticipate trouble and make the first move, we put ourselves in the right with our Roman brethren?
Caiaphas Precisely.
Annas Dear me! You know sometimes you remind me of myself when young. I was noted for exceptional mental agility. Do you think I could have my dinner? At my age I find these pyrotechnics very exhausting.
Caiaphas Father Annas?
Annas My son?
Caiaphas You don't think he is Messiah, do you?
Annas Good gracious no! A revelation of that magnitude would come through the properly regulated channels . . . and that, of course—is us! What an uncomfortable thought! I'm far too old to face that sort of thing. (*As he goes out*) As a matter of reference, I *shall* enter that money as having been paid. It's all in the family.

BLACK-OUT

CURTAIN

ACT II

Thomas again appears as formerly

Thomas The pity of it is that you people are seeing all the black side of it. You're bound to get the wrong impression of those years and especially Judas. Still, it's too late now. There's no going back. Of course, the rest of us didn't know what was going on at this time we're showing you. If Judas had only had the sense to put into words whatever was bothering him. If he'd only *talked* to him! He was never difficult to talk to. But perhaps Jesus was proud as well. He must have known what Judas was thinking, and maybe he knew Judas had to work it out for himself. We were really all as bad, because none of us understood what he was up to . . . Anyway, there was this awful tension in the air. Judas would go out of his way to avoid Jesus one minute, and hang around him the next, and all the time he went on trying to persuade him to get out of Jerusalem . . . "Go back to Galilee, have a nice quiet rest," he kept on saying, and he went on and on about wanting to go fishing, which was funny, because he was always sea-sick when we took him. Then came that night . . . the night I shall remember for ever . . .

He walks away. Spot goes off him and stage lights go up

SCENE 1

An upper room in an inn in Jerusalem. Throughout this scene there is a terrible sense of urgency on the part of Jesus; he speaks very quickly. They are coming to the end of a meal, all twelve are together. Jesus is in the centre with Judas on his left and John on his right.

Jesus Have any of you got swords?
Peter (*astonished*) No, Master.
Jesus Then buy some. Have we money, Judas?
Judas Yes.
Jesus Very well then.
John What do we want them for?
Jesus You may need to defend yourselves, to *defend* yourselves remember. Can you get them this time of the night?
Peter Yes, the Bazaar's still open.

There is general consternation. Judas looks sick

Jesus We'll finish our meal first. This is the last Passover I shall eat with you, and afterwards we'll walk together in the garden for the last time. (*He looks quite deliberately at Judas, who looks frightened as well as sick*)
Judas What's the matter?

Peter You're talking in riddles.

Jesus (*very earnestly*) Listen to me . . . listen to me, all of you. Time is running out. There's no time left now for you to argue or me to convince, so you *must* listen to me, and you must believe me. I've got to leave you, and there are things I must say to you.

Thomas Are you going away without us?

Jesus Yes, without you.

Peter You can't spring it on us just like that!

Jesus (*another look at Judas*) I think perhaps the timing has been taken out of my hands.

Judas (*in a panic*) No one will hurt you; there is no one who would dare.

John (*in a panic for a different reason*) We've been with you such a long time. I for one can't imagine my life without you. Where would we go now?

James What will we do? We've been with you for three years.

Jesus (*very urgently*) Listen to me—all of you! Nothing . . . nothing can separate you from me. It may be that because of me you'll have to face things you never expected, but remember and remember this always, between us, you and I, we can overcome the world! (*Laughs with the old enthusiasm for living*) More than that, far more than that, we can turn the world upside down!

Judas (*quietly*) If anything happened to you, it would destroy me.

Jesus (*emphatically*) No!—no one can destroy you, nothing can destroy you, you can only destroy yourselves. Remember this, too—I don't promise that you won't know misery and pain and death, but I *do* promise you that none of these things can destroy you if you don't want them to. You came from God. You are his Sons, you can go back to him if you choose. No power on earth or in hell can prevent that.

John What must we do? What do you want us to do?

Jesus Stay together. Work together. Heal the sick. Look after the poor. Give comfort to the lonely and the lost. Love one another. Be just and kind to your enemies and never, never be afraid. Peter!

Peter Yes, Master?

Jesus Forgive one another *everything*—(*He smiles*)—not just seven times, seventy times seven!

Peter Yes, yes, I'll remember.

Jesus And one thing more—think about this—no man shows greater love than he who will lay down his life for another.

Thomas (*shattering the emotional tension*) I don't understand all this! Oh yes I understand the words and their meaning, but I don't understand the necessity for them. I don't know what all this is about. I don't see how anything can happen to you if we don't leave you, and of course we won't.

Peter (*much relieved*) Of course we won't. Nothing can happen while you're with us. We'd follow you to the world's end if need be, and beyond. I'd go anywhere with you, even to prison and death!

Jesus (*looking at him thoughtfully*) Would you, Peter?

Peter Can you doubt it? We all would.

Thomas If we aren't loyal to you, who will be?

Jesus Who indeed? (*He looks round at them all, still thoughtful, and then drops his bomb*) And yet, before this long night's over there are some here who will betray me.

There are loud protests from all but Judas. All look shocked.

Peter (*very upset and annoyed*) That's a terrible thing to say. Who would do that?

Jesus (*very quietly*) You for one!

Peter Me? God of Israel! How can you bring yourself to think it, let alone say it?

Judas (*whispers, tortured*) Who else? (*Jesus looks at him and says nothing*)

Thomas Let's get out of this blasted city! I hate the set-up here. The Temple police are everywhere, snooping and listening. Let's go back to Galilee and lie low for a while.

Peter What's that supposed to mean—"lie low"? We're not criminals or bandits.

Thomas Nobody said we were but we could all do with a break. Let's go back in the morning.

John This time tomorrow we could be out at sea.

James (*excited*) We could even go up into Syria for the summer.

John Let's go back tonight. We don't have to wait till tomorrow.

Peter We could take Mary's family with us. They can stay with my mother.

Judas hasn't had an answer to his question—he is in mental torment. Throughout this conversation Jesus has been watching him steadily

Judas (*whispering*) You didn't answer me. Who else?

Jesus (*quietly*) One of you who will eat from this dish. (*Passes it all round the table, first to Judas*)

John Master, do we go tonight? We could be away in an hour.

Jesus (*after long pause*) I have business here in Jerusalem. You can go. I'll think of you there with the boats and the sea . . .

Judas Why don't *you* go? Why don't we all go?

Jesus It's too late.

John But is this the end? I mean, the end of us together?

Jesus (*walking to side of stage*) I didn't say that. (*Pause*) No. It isn't the end. Wait for me. One day I'll come along the shore to meet you. (*He gets up, walks to the front of the stage; he looks unhappy and weary*)

Judas follows him; he, too, is in a turmoil. He touches Jesus on the arm

Judas Jesus! Master! (*Jesus says nothing*) Will you excuse me? I'm not well.

Jesus (*looks suddenly stricken*) Judas! Let's get this over. If you ever loved me, what you're going to do, do it quickly.

Judas throws his hands out in a gesture of despair. Things have gone badly wrong

Judas For the love of God, go back to Galilee. (*He starts to go*)
Jesus Judas!
Judas Yes?
Jesus When it's all over, don't look back, carry on . . . I shall need you . . .
Judas No one will hurt you!

Judas exits, almost in tears

Thomas What was all that about? Is he ill? Shall I go after him?
Jesus No. Leave him alone. He chooses his own way—as we all do.
John Something dreadful's going to happen. I can feel it.
Jesus (*walks behind them back to his place—with his hands first on one man's shoulder, then another*) Don't be afraid, not of people, or of ideas, or of things. Fear shrivels up the soul, paralyses the will, poisons the mind. Remember, you can conquer the world if you're not afraid. (*He returns to the table, sits down again*) One more thing. You may not understand what I'm going to do now, but you will. Look! (*He takes bread from a basket in front of him*) Eat with me once more. This is my body broken for you, and this—(*He takes the communal cup of wine from in front of him and spills a drop on the floor*)—this is my blood spilt for you. In the future when you meet to have a meal together, do this and remember me and the fellowship we shared.

Peter has had enough; he jumps up, goes to Jesus, holds him, and says violently

Peter Stop it! For God's sake stop it! What are you talking about? You're not ill, are you? You're only thirty, what's this talk of dying? Who wants to kill you? I've told you, we've all told you, nothing can happen to you. We're ready to follow you—anywhere. We'll look after you.
Jesus We shall see.

BLACK-OUT

SCENE 2

Later the same night

The garden of Gethsemane. It is dark. Three disciples are asleep on the ground. Jesus is talking. Any composure he shows before other people has gone. This is the soul of the man revealed

Jesus Father! . . . The hour brought me here, but I haven't finished . . . give me time . . . I must have more time . . . Just this *one* thing . . . I let you shut everything out . . . you took me over completely. I walked on the mountains and your voice filled the world . . . nothing mattered as much . . . no one became as important . . . I'm not complaining . . . you were enough . . . far, far more than enough . . . but these are my friends . . . don't overestimate me . . . I love

them more than that . . . I *need* them . . . their need of me makes
me strong. I'm not ready to leave them . . . Father! Just a little more
time . . . a year! Another year . . . that's all . . . I'll accept it then
. . . I promise you . . . I've done everything you asked of me . . .
please . . . please let this cup pass from me, please . . . (*Long pause*)
My heart is breaking . . . oh God! They're not ready to be left. (*Silence
darkness, a great struggle, and finally self-control*) . . . So be it . . .
what you want . . . (*He moves over to the sleeping disciples, stands
looking down at them, stoops and touches John. Jesus speaks quietly*) Oh
God! help me through this! John! John! Peter! (*No response*) Couldn't
you stop awake with me just for an hour? Poor lads, how will you face
the rest? There's not been enough time . . .

*There is the sound of many voices, flame of torches, tramping feet; a
contingent of the Temple Guards enter with a few civilians, including Judas.
Everyone is armed to the teeth. This brings Jesus back to his usual self-
mastery and authority. He is poised and cynically amused by the battery of
weapons brought out against him*

1st Guard Squad, halt! Here they are!
2nd Guard Is that *all* there are?

The disciples get up, dazed and not fully comprehending

1st Guard Come on, up with you! On your feet.
Jesus What do you want?
1st Guard We're looking for a man. Jesus of Nazareth.
Jesus Well, you've found him.
Peter You'll regret it if you come any closer. Leave us alone.
2nd Guard Nothing personal, mate. We're obeying orders.
Jesus Whose orders?
1st Guard Orders from my lord Caiaphas, High Priest of Israel.
James (*spots Judas lurking in background*) Judas! They've arrested Judas!
2nd Guard (*making a sudden grab at Peter*) Come on, you. We'll take the
  lot of you, then we'll know we've got the right one.
Peter (*struggling furiously*) Let me go.
2nd Guard Come quietly and you won't get hurt.

*Peter suddenly becomes quiet. The soldier is off his guard. Peter whips his own
sword out and brandishes it. The guards turn nasty. Jesus puts down Peter's
arm*

Jesus (*with tremendous authority*) Put up your swords . . . all of you!

*There is a moment of astounded silence, then astonishingly, one by one, they
all put away their swords*

Now then—am I a criminal or a bandit that you come out with swords
and staves to arrest me?

There is a silence, they all look sheepish

Well—I'm here. What are you afraid of? That I'll call down legions of angels, or was it devils, to help me?

1st Guard Now look—it's nothing to do with us. Like I said, we only act under orders, and like my friend told you, it's nothing personal.

Jesus Why come out like thieves in the night to find me? Every day this week I've been in the Temple quite openly.

2nd Guard We're only obeying instructions. Will you come with us, sir?

Jesus (*smiling*) I have a choice?

2nd Guard No, sir.

Jesus Very well, then. I'm ready.

1st Guard Just a moment! That won't do. (*Jesus stands waiting with raised eyebrows*)

2nd Guard What's the matter now?

1st Guard My lord Caiaphas said we must be certain to get positive identification.

2nd Guard Well, it's obvious this is the right man.

1st Guard Yes—but we don't know for sure.

2nd Guard Oh well! (*Shouting*) Iscariot! Where's the man Iscariot?

Judas hangs back. Someone shoves him forward

Come on! You said you'd be responsible for establishing identity. Now point him out.

Judas I made no bargain that involved soldiers and arms.

The disciples look at him astounded

1st Guard Come on! You've been paid well for it, I hear.

John Judas! Oh God! I saw this coming.

Peter Bloody traitor! (*Tries to get at him*)

1st Guard (*bawling at Judas*) Get on with it!

Judas walks slowly to Jesus, eyes fixed on him, then his arms go round him. Jesus returns the embrace. It may be in theory the kiss of betrayal, but in practice it turns out to be the last desperate embrace of close and dear friends

Jesus (*whispering*) So. This is it.

Peter Let me get at him.

There is a scuffle, two soldiers grab him, another Guard forcibly removes Judas, two more Guards take Jesus—an escort forms round him

Jesus Let the others go. You have no quarrel with them.

2nd Guard I'm not so sure about that.

1st Guard Oh, let's not stand here all night. We had no instructions about them.

2nd Guard All right. Let them go. Now then, if you don't want to be arrested—clear off!

1st Guard Judas Iscariot, you'd better come with us. You'll be wanted as a witness.

Judas (*shouting*) I won't testify!

1st Guard (*grinning*) You can please yourself. If you stay here, your friends will probably lynch you! Squad, march! Left! Right! Left! Right!

They march out as lights fade to a

BLACK-OUT

Thomas enters

Thomas I'm ashamed to say that when we heard he'd been arrested, we ran away. I'm telling you because sooner or later you're bound to wonder what we were all doing when they took him, and I dare say you'll remember all our fine promises to him. We didn't exactly run away. We melted into the background, as it were. You see, we thought they'd round up the rest of us, but they didn't bother. They'd got him and I suppose they thought that would be the end of it, or maybe they suspected we'd be nothing without him, and they were right, at that time. We were cowards, I suppose, but before you condemn us too harshly— think! What would you have done? Up to the last minute, we couldn't believe anything like that would really happen. In a way we were disappointed in him. In fact, I was angry with him because he'd let it happen. We didn't know what to do. One day he was making fun of us, and he said we were like a lot of silly sheep without a shepherd, and that's about it! It was all right him saying, "Don't be frightened", but when he wasn't there it was a different story altogether. Anyway, that's how it happened that none of us were at the trial, if you could call it a trial . . .

Walks off. Lights come up on the stage

SCENE 3

Later the same night. The Council Chambers of the great Sanhedrin in the Temple. There ought to be a large convocation of seventy, but there was no time to summon them together. Annas, Caiaphas, Joseph of Arimathea, Shadrach, Jacob-ben-levi, these few represent the many. Caiaphas sits on a throne at the top of a flight of steps. The others sit at each side on different levels

Caiaphas Are all the witnesses present?

Jacob As many as could be found at such short notice, my lord Caiaphas. We also arrested the Bethany household where the prisoner was staying.

Joseph That's stretching the law a bit. Was it necessary?

Jacob Well, I thought it was a good idea. It can do no harm to question them. They might even be persuaded to testify against him to save their own skins.

Caiaphas There are no charges against them, of course, but they can't be sure of that. We can certainly use them. Is Judas Iscariot here?

Jacob He's no use. He refused to testify, sir.

Caiaphas Refused?
Jacob Yes, sir.
Caiaphas Where is he?
Jacob Well, he's in the antechamber, but I'm not quite sure what he's doing there.
Caiaphas See that he's brought in with the other witnesses.
Jacob (*goes to the wings and shouts*) Bring the prisoner in!
Annas (*aside to Caiaphas*) I think it's a great pity you didn't keep Judas out of it.

Jesus is brought in by the two Temple Guards. They are accompanied by witnesses. There are two men and two women together with Judas, Martha, Mary and a young man. They all sit on benches except Jesus. His behaviour throughout the trial is fascinating and unexpected. He persists in finding it all irrelevant and rather entertaining

Caiaphas (*after a long look at Jesus which he returns with interest*) Hm! You're not quite what I expected. It's a pity we have to come face to face under these circumstances. I'm told you're a very interesting young man.
Annas (*peevishly*) He's a very foolish young man. He has caused us a great deal of trouble. What have you got to say for yourself? (*Jesus says nothing but eyes Annas with interest. The Priest looks uncomfortable*) Now! Now! We are being indulgent with you and inviting you to explain yourself. Speak up, my boy! (*Jesus is still silent. He has a long look at Jacob, Joseph, Shadrach. After all, they are old acquaintances. The Priests look perplexed. They look at each other*) He's being insolent! That won't get you anywhere. (*Jesus smiles at Annas with great charm. Annas looks flustered*)
Caiaphas Don't you intend to say anything?
Jesus Am I on trial?
Caiaphas What do you mean?
Jesus What I said. Am I on trial?
Caiaphas Well, in a manner of speaking, I suppose you are.
Judas (*shouts out*) What for? This is not just!
Annas Be quiet!
Jesus I have nothing to say.
Caiaphas Why not?
Jesus As I understand the law, the trial is not legal.

Caiaphas and Annas look at each other, unsure of themselves

Annas If we say it's legal, it's legal.
Jesus (*smiling*) That's a new definition of the law.
Annas He's being deliberately offensive.
Caiaphas To what do you object?
Jesus In the first place only a few of you are here. Worthy men no doubt— (*Shadrach, Jacob, Joseph exchange looks*)—but still an insufficient number for a legal trial. In the second place you are not allowed to hold a court of inquiry by night.

Annas (*very irritable*) Are you teaching us our jobs? Coming from you, this is perverse to say the least.

Jesus (*quietly*) You asked me.

Shadrach gives him a good swipe across the mouth

Shadrach That's to teach you respect when you talk to a High Priest. (*Jesus looks at him . . . Shadrach looks uncomfortable, puts his hand to his head, turns to Annas*) May I have permission to sit for a moment? The heat! I feel unwell.

Annas nods his head graciously, Shadrach sits, mopping his brow

Annas We all know how much respect your high and mightiness has for the law.

Caiaphas (*courteously, trying to bring the situation back on the rails*) I assure you I have the full authority of the Sanhedrin behind me. Any decision we make here will be endorsed by all of them. (*Murmurs of assent*) Please proceed with the charges.

Jacob Jesus-bar-Joseph, late of Nazareth now of no fixed abode, you are accused on three counts: witchcraft, heresy, insurrection!

Jesus again smiles. The idea that he is in league with the Devil never fails to amuse him

Annas Call the first witness!

Jacob pushes forward the dancing girl Miriam

Now! We have spent some time and thought compiling an accurate dossier on the prisoner, so you need not trouble yourself to tell lies on his account. I understand you have circulated some story about an incident that happened at your wedding? Something to do with magic . . .

Girl Well . . .

Caiaphas (*kindly*) Tell the court your name.

Girl Miriam, sir.

Caiaphas Very well then, Miriam. Father Annas has asked you a question.

Miriam It wasn't a story, sir, it was true. But I don't know whether it was magic or not.

Annas (*majestically*) That is for the court to decide. Tell us what happened.

Miriam We invited him to our wedding. We know his mother very well. In fact, she was helping us with the food. He brought a lot of his friends with him. We didn't mind that at all, only the wine ran out.

There is laughter in the court

Annas Very distressing. Mind you, it has previously been brought to our attention that the prisoner and his associates are given to indulging themselves on these occasions. What happened next?

Miriam I was standing next to his mother. She said to him, "What a shame! Can't you do something to help them?" Well at first he looked upset, angry even, and he said something to her I didn't catch. Then he must have changed his mind because quite suddenly he laughed and all

his friends laughed, and then he told the servants to fill up our big water
jugs.

Caiaphas What with?

Miriam Oh, water, of course. Only when they carried them to the table . . .
it was wine!

Reactions—gasps, laughs, scorn, etc.

Caiaphas You are quite sure about this?

Miriam Positive, sir. He said we mustn't tell anyone, but it saved the
situation. Anyway, it was better wine than we had in the first place.

Shadrach (*waspishly*) My lord Caiaphas—may I suggest that by that stage
they would all be incapable of knowing what they were drinking anyway? . . .

*There is more laughter from the court. Another look from Jesus seems to
unnerve Shadrach*

Annas Mumbo-Jumbo! They tell me the prisoner spent some time in
Egypt. He's picked up some of their tricks. Sorcery's a profession with
them.

Caiaphas On this charge of necromancy there are two other incidents for
us to consider before coming to any conclusions. The next witness,
please!

*A man about thirty years of age is pushed forward by Jacob. He is defiant,
cheeky, probably to cover a certain amount of fear*

Man Don't shove me about like that. I came of my own free will, didn't I?

Annas To testify against the prisoner? (*Again Jesus looks amused*)

Man (*indignant*) Certainly not! I'm for him!

Annas Dear me! There seems to be some mistake here.

Caiaphas If you would be good enough to leave this to me, Father Annas?
I know what I'm doing. Now, sir, you are a professional beggar?

Man Well, I used to be. Mind you, I wouldn't call it a profession, more of
a necessity. I had my pitch at the corner of the Temple steps; everybody
knows me. (*He grins round at the court*)

Caiaphas Quite so. Now, why is it no longer essential for you to pursue
this—career?

Man I couldn't work you see, I've been blind all my life. I'm not just a
layabout. (*Piously*) God in his infinite mercy saw fit to lay this great
affliction on me.

Caiaphas Well?

Man Oh, I thought you knew. Yes, well, last week a man gave me back my
sight.

Annas If God, as you say, made you blind, then no one had a right to
cure you!

Caiaphas Please! Father Annas! Tell me, my good man, *how* did this
person restore your sight?

Man I don't know really. I felt his hands touch my eyes and then he told
me to go and wash my face.

Annas Just like that?
Man Yes.

Annas snorts

Caiaphas And what day was this?
Man Oh, it was the Sabbath! The better the day, the better the deed, I always say. (*He grins all round again*)
Annas Be silent! Nobody wants to hear your inane comments; they detract from the gravity of the charge.
Shadrach (*viciously*) That's typical of him, trouble-maker. Why couldn't he have cured him some other day of the week? He is a notorious Sabbath-breaker, and a bad man. So how can he have healed you?
Man I don't know. All I know is that I *was* blind and for the first time in thirty years I can see! It's a funny thing that this bad man could cure me, and all you good, holy men couldn't!
Annas (*very cross*) If you persist in these lies and profanities, you will be excommunicated.
Joseph Do you think this could be a conspiracy? Have we proof that the man really was blind?
Jacob (*beckons a woman from the benches*) Here's his mother.
Caiaphas There's no need to be alarmed. Tell the truth and no one will hurt you. What is your name?
Woman Rachel, sir.
Annas (*ponderously*) This is a very serious matter indeed, and you must take care how you answer. Now, look at him and think very carefully before you reply—do you know this man?
Rachel (*bursts out laughing*) I ought to, he's my son. No-good scamp! If I don't know him, nobody does. Nothing but trouble since the day he was born.
Annas Was he blind?
Rachel (*carefully*) Oh yes, always, all his life.
Caiaphas Was he cured by Jesus of Nazareth?
Rachel (*wary now*) I don't know anythihg about that.
Caiaphas Do you *know* Jesus of Nazareth?
Rachel Oh no, sir. I don't know anyone; I keep out of trouble.

Jesus is very amused by this pair of comedians

Annas You've got a bright pair here!
Caiaphas (*beginning to lose patience*) Do you know that your son is no longer blind?
Rachel So he says!
Caiaphas So he says? Don't you believe him, then?
Rachel I don't know anything about it, sir.
Annas Tell me, my good woman, how could a man who defies our law and sets himself against the teaching of the Elders perform so great a miracle?
Rachel I don't know, but it would have been better if he'd stayed blind than displease all you clever and godly gentlemen!
Man (*quite good-humoured*) Silly bitch!

Annas (*thundering*) Be silent! It is written "Thou shalt honour thy father and thy mother". This man's pernicious teaching will corrupt the world!

Joseph Aren't you glad your son has got back his sight?

Rachel Oh yes, sir, but you see he hasn't a trade, he doesn't go to the Temple any more and he always seems to be under my feet. And of course he doesn't bring any money home.

Caiaphas (*to man*) Are you quite sure that you can see?

The Man looks round the court fairly slowly, then making up his mind, on one swift movement he goes to Jesus and kneels at his feet, kisses his hands. There is an uproar, the Priests are very annoyed

Annas Throw him out! He's an imbecile.

Shadrach and Jacob haul him to his feet and hustle him out

Caiaphas (*troubled*) He exerts a very sinister influence on people, very sinister indeed. (*Jesus looks bored*) Now, the last witness on this issue, please. Martha, daughter of him they call Simon the leper of Bethany, will you step forward?

Martha (*very dignified*) I don't wish to testify, my lord Caiaphas.

Caiaphas (*gently*) No one is going to distress you. We only want a little co-operation.

Martha (*firmly*) I will not testify against him.

Caiaphas We shall not ask you to do that. Answer these questions truthfully, that's all.

She looks at Jesus—he nods

Martha What do you want to know?

Caiaphas You have a brother called Lazarus?

Martha (*after a pause*) Yes.

Caiaphas Jesus of Nazareth is said to have cured him. Tell us about it.

Martha (*very reluctant*) Jesus asked us not to talk about it, sir.

Caiaphas Did he indeed? I'm afraid on this occasion we must overrule his wishes. Honest men are not afraid when their deeds see the light of day. Tell us about it.

Martha (*finding this very difficult*) . . . My brother died, sir.

Caiaphas I see. So Jesus did *not* cure him?

Martha He was buried, sir . . . four days. He died. (*She shuts up abruptly*)

Caiaphas I can't hear you. Speak up! I'm afraid I don't understand you. How can Jesus have cured him if your poor brother died?

Martha (*whispering*) He brought him back . . . they opened the grave . . . he came out.

Gasps, protests, etc., from the court

Annas Come now, my girl. You're asking rather a lot of us; you can't really expect us to believe that.

Martha (*simply*) Many people saw it. All our household knew, they had *seen*, that he was dead. I told you, he was in the grave four days.

Caiaphas This may be so, but I have it on good authority that Lazarus

has not been seen since this one dramatic appearance. What have you
to say to that?

Again, Jesus finds the proceedings amusing

Annas (*gleefully*) Yes, why has this resurrected brother not been seen
about?
Martha He was very tired, and he has been resting. He cannot bear to be
stared at.

Loud guffaws, laughter, "He should be in a circus . . ." etc., etc.

Annas This sounds a very tall story altogether.
Martha (*pause*) He is here *now*, sir.
Annas I beg your pardon? What did you say?
Martha He is here now, sir.

*Lazarus, smiling, moves up to stand by Martha. He puts his arm round her.
Moment of dead silence followed by uproar. Caiaphas holds up his hands until
there is silence again. Lazarus and Jesus exchange grins*

Annas You stand there and expect us to believe you were once dead?
Lazarus They tell me that I was, sir. I believe them.
Annas You look very much alive to me. Tell me now, what was it like
being dead?
Lazarus (*there is a long pause then he speaks with sincerity*) I don't know.
Which were dreams and which was death, how can I know? But I know
this—this I remember. At the last, he brought me back from a place I'd
never been to before, and yet I'd always known it. I don't think I wanted
to come back.

Again Jesus smiles, and Lazarus looks at him intently

Annas (*breaking the tension*) Clearly this man did not die. It is a hoax, a
plot to make the court look ridiculous.
Caiaphas (*disturbed*) Perhaps he was unconscious. I don't feel these young
people are lying deliberately.
Shadrach (*clearly he hates Jesus—could it be something personal?*) It's
another example of the way he plays upon the ignorance of the people.
He has mastered some black art which produces illusions and hallucina-
tions. I think the first charge has been proved beyond any doubt.
Jacob I agree. He's obviously a wizard; he exerts strange influences over
people.

*As Jacob says this, Shadrach is whispering something to Annas; whatever it
is, Annas is very gleeful*

Annas Just a moment before you two go. Isn't the girl they call Mary of
Magdala your sister?
Martha (*reluctant*) . . . Yes, sir.
Annas I thought so. (*Very smooth*) This court has no doubt heard of the
lady in question.

Laughter, whispering, etc. Mary holds her head up and looks extremely haughty

Now, you shall have the pleasure of meeting her.

Shadrach goes to fetch her, she puts aside his arm, not nastily but deliberately, she joins Martha and Lazarus. Annas changes his tone and bawls now

Is it not a fact that you are the favourite prostitute of the Roman legionaries in Israel?

Mary (*dignity*) Wrong on two counts, my lord.

Annas Indeed?

Mary In the first place I am no longer the favourite prostitute of the Roman legionaries, and in the second place, that I ever achieved such a unique distinction is highly questionable. I had rivals.

There is laughter

Annas (*feeling the game is slipping away*) That's as may be. Is it not a fact that you are now an intimate friend of the prisoner?

There is more laughter. Mary gives Jesus a long look, which he returns. It is as though they two are in the room together and alone

Mary I would be proud to think that I was his friend. I gave up the way of life you accuse me of because of him.

Annas . . . You preferred him to all the others?

Mary (*after a pause*) You might put it like that—yes.

Annas (*quietly*) Do you love him?

Jacob Why hasn't he married? It is a good young Jew's duty to marry and have sons. Isn't he normal?

Annas (*persistent*) Do you love him?

Mary (*pause*) Yes.

Annas (*shouting*) Aren't you ashamed of yourself?

Mary No . . . Proud.

Annas If he's so concerned for your welfare, why doesn't he marry you?

Mary It's not that kind of love.

There are rude noises, etc.

Annas Come now, knowing what sort of a girl you are, do you expect us to believe that? (*She is silent*)

Jacob I asked you a question. Why hasn't he married? If not you, someone else?

Mary (*quite simply*) He's too busy.

Laughter. Jesus, too, finds this amusing

Caiaphas Tell me, my dear, one more question—does he love you?

Mary (*after another very long look exchanged with Jesus*) I don't know.

Caiaphas (*very bland*) Thank you. You three have been very helpful. We want nothing more from you for the present.

They go back to their seats

Now then, we will proceed to the charge of insurrection . . . this will not take long. This man preached peace and the love of God, and the love of one's neighbour, up and down the length and breadth of this land.

I can only conclude that this was a deliberate attempt to allay suspicion and to rouse confidence in himself. Because last week, throwing pretence aside, he rode in triumph into our city, and the people shouted, "Hosanna, King of the Jews!" He did not contradict them.

Joseph (*laboriously and pedantically*) May I point out, my lord Caiaphas, that he rode on a mule, not on a horse, so we must be fair here—to ride on a mule was not a declaration of violent intent. Now, had it been a horse, that would have been a clear demonstration of motives that were basically warlike . . .

Annas (*cross*) Whose side are you on, Joseph? If you can't be more helpfully constructive than that, keep quiet. (*Yet another smile from Jesus infuriates him*) All you're doing is entertaining the prisoner. In fact, he's the only one who seems to be getting any enjoyment out of these proceedings.

Caiaphas (*plodding on*) He allowed the crowds to give him the greeting reserved for a king, and in the very precincts of the Temple he indulged in a violent display of temper and did considerable damage to property.

Joseph What damage did he do?

Caiaphas (*very patient*) He threw over the money-changers' tables and in the confusion some of the livestock got away.

There is laughter

Annas It was not funny. It was disgraceful. Goats and birds all over the place!

More laughter

Joseph (*quite heated*) I'll tell you what is disgraceful, the way these money-changers cheat the Gentiles out of a fair rate of exchange. They give the country a bad name.

Caiaphas There is worse to come if you will be patient a little longer. Will the witness who heard his threat to destroy Jerusalem come forward and confront the court with her evidence?

The other dancing girl, Salome, now comes forward

Salome (*very dignified*) I'm here, my lord Caiaphas. I remember the claims well because of the gravity of their nature. I regret to say that he stated quite definitely that he had come to bring not peace, but the sword. There can be no mistake about this; he said he would set brother against brother, father against son. He went so far as to declare that not a stone in Jerusalem would be left standing, and that he would destroy the Temple. (*She sits down—hubbub as everyone thinks of the implications*)

Caiaphas You heard all this for yourself.

Salome (*bobbing up*) Yes.

Judas That's a lie! This woman is jealous of Mary. He would hever have said things like that to strangers.

Joseph I happen to know that when he talked about the destruction of the Temple he was not talking about *this* Temple.

Annas (*very furious*) This is too bad, Joseph! You are obstructing the course of justice.

Joseph (*obstinately*) You must give him a fair trial.

Annas Are you suggesting he's not getting one?

Caiaphas Gentlemen! Friends! We must not lose confidence in each other, or the very foundations of the Temple will be shaken! I think this person's evidence, brief though it is, in its implications has amply supported the charge of inciting rebellion. Now to the gravest crime of all, and one I'm afraid that cannot be overlooked, or refuted, that of blasphemy. Again and again, in the presence of many witnesses, he has deliberately overruled the Mosaic Code, thus by obvious inference, establishing himself as a superior authority. In fact—and here I am at a loss for words—he has made statements which can only be interpreted as a deluded identification of himself with the One Living God! (*Gasps*) This is pathetic, for he is young and talented, but it is also monstrous and evil and must be destroyed. We have here in this court a man who has listened carefully to him over the past months and is prepared to repeat some of the more diabolical and perverted of his statements. Will the witness step forward?

He does so

Will you repeat the words you have already quoted to me?

Man My lord Caiaphas! On separate occasions, of which I can give you the dates, he has said the following: No. 1 "No man comes to the Father except by me." No. 2 "I am the Resurrection and the life, he who believes in me, though he were dead, yet shall he live." No. 3 "I and my Father are one." No. 4 "You who have seen me, have seen the Father."

There is silence, then an uproar, cries of "Blasphemy! Heresy! Stone him!" etc.

Caiaphas (*raising voice above the clamour*) I charge you by Almighty God, do you know the penalty for the unspeakable sin of blasphemy in the Mosaic Code?

Judas (*shouting*) This is not justice! These are things he said to *us* his friends! They must not be taken out of context.

Caiaphas (*ignoring the interruption*) Must I repeat the question? Do you know the penalty?

Jesus Yes, I know it.

Caiaphas Are you guilty or not guilty?

Jesus Of blasphemy? Not guilty.

Caiaphas Are you Messiah?

Jesus If I tell you, you will not belive me.

Caiaphas By the Living God I charge you to tell me; as you will answer on the dreadful day of judgement—are you Messiah?

Jesus (*pause*) I am!

Loud uproar

Caiaphas (*wearily*) You condemn yourself out of your own mouth.

Joseph (*shouting*) That isn't legal! It is not enough for a prisoner to condemn *himself*. All witnesses must agree on all counts . . . I will have no further part in these abominable proceedings. I quit the court.

Joseph exits in fury

Caiaphas If you try him again, in any other way, there can only be one
outcome.
Judas I protest! I have heard him say repeatedly, "You are all Sons of
God!" If he imputes Divinity to himself, so he does to all of us!
Caiaphas What is the verdict of this court? Guilty or not guilty?

*There are roars from the pro-Priests of "Guilty, he must die, stone the heretic",
etc. Loud protests from anti-Priests and screams of protest from Mary and
Martha*

Clear the court! Clear this court!

*In confusion, shoved and pushed by the Temple Guards, all depart. Judas
sinks down, stunned by the swift passage of events. Caiaphas remains looking
at him. At last Judas rises and slowly goes to him puts his hands out in
appeal, but has lost use of his tongue*

Well—you caused us some embarassment!
Judas (*whisper*) You gave me no idea . . . no idea . . . this . . . it
could come to this.
Caiaphas (*bland*) It was inevitable.
Judas He has done *nothing* to deserve death. What's more, everyone in
their right mind knows it. What will happen now?
Caiaphas (*patiently*) He will go before the procurator first thing in the
morning; fortunately he is in Jerusalem. With luck it will all be over by
this time tomorrow.
Judas (*silent with unbelief and horror*) All . . . over? No! But he is a
completely innocent man. You have betrayed me. You told me no harm
would come to him.
Caiaphas (*quite kind now things have gone his way*) By way of consolation,
let me say this to you. That young man has known perfectly well all
along where he was going. The verdict was no surprise to him. Let us say
indeed that it was of his own choosing.
Judas (*passionately*) What good is it to him or to anyone else that he
should die? He has done nothing to deserve this. You don't understand,
he is a *good* man.
Caiaphas He is a dangerous one.
Judas Why do you hate him? What has he done to you?
Caiaphas (*surprised*) I don't hate him. Whatever gave you that idea? I
rather liked him! However, sometimes it is expedient that one man should
die for the people, better that than see a whole nation perish.
Judas I don't understand you.

Caiaphas looks at him, then goes out

BLACK-OUT

CURTAIN

ACT III

Scene 1

Early the following morning. The Governor's house in Jerusalem. Pontius Pilate, if not in a downright bad mood, is at least extremely harassed. He is dressing, not assisted by his wife Claudia Procula, who is upsetting him

Pilate (*growling*) Why they want me to see him at the crack of dawn I can't imagine. They're up to no good. It's one of their sneaky ways of getting round something or other.

Claudia (*wearily*) That's obvious. It's their Passover, after today they wouldn't be able to do anything to him for at least a week. *Please* don't support them in this. Refuse to try him.

Pilate (*exasperated*) On what justifiable grounds? You've lived with me long enough to know my feelings about women who try to interfere in administration. When it comes to politics you're an addle-headed lot. Now go back to bed and let me get on with my job.

Claudia I can't go back to bed.

Pilate (*looking round for some items of equipment*) Now where did I put that belt? (*Looks around vaguely. Claudia finds it for him.*) Ah yes—there it is. Go on—there's a good girl. You're distracting me.

Claudia Darling! I'm not being stupid about this. I *can't* go to sleep again; I *dread* going to sleep.

Pilate (*stands stock-still and looks at her*) What on earth are you talking about?

Claudia I told you. It's that dream; I have it every night . . . it terrifies me.

Pilate Look! You know it's only a dream—shake it off.

Claudia I *can't*! That's just it.

Pilate (*rooting around for a scroll on his writing table which he glances through quickly*) Well, go and find something to do; forget it!

Claudia looks hurt and upset, and in the end Pilate gives in

All right, then—tell me about it, but hurry up.

Claudia (*as her speech goes on, she is lost in her own emotions*) It starts with a feeling of coldness—terrible cold. I can't stop shivering and I'm crying, too, but I don't know why. My heart is breaking with grief . . . I'm so drowned in sadness, I can't tell you, and I'm all by myself. I look round, and I'm in a vast, desolate place, a great empty grey waste, grey dust, grey sky. Suddenly in the distance I hear a strange kind of murmur and it grows louder and louder until it's roaring in my ears . . . Time goes by, I don't know how long, but I realize that this murmur is made up of many voices throbbing around me, in me, from all directions. But instead of being glad that I can hear other voices, other people in this desolation, I am mortally afraid, and I try to run headlong from them. But they hound me, pursue me, voices of young men, old men, young girls, old women, voices of clamouring crowds, solitary, desperate voices, voices of children—for some reason they horrify me most, and I put my hands to my ears to shut them out, and I scream for pity, but they don't stop—they go on and on and on.

Pilate What do they say?

Claudia That's just it. They say your name!

Pilate (*absolutely mystified*) My name? What's so terrifying about that?

Claudia It's a kind of chant, an endless, monotonous chant. I can hear it now . . . expressionless . . . passionless . . . as though *you* don't matter . . . as though you're not a person any more, not the man I love.

Pilate You're being obscure! What do they say?

Claudia . . . It doesn't make sense, "Suffered under Pontius Pilate, suffered under Pontius Pilate, suffered under Pontius Pilate" (*voice rises . . .*) Please—*please*, don't have anything to do with this . . . I *know* there's some connection.

Pilate (*uneasy*) Because my wife has a dream I must alter my routines, my duties?

Claudia It's too real to be only a dream. It's some dreadful omen the gods have sent.

Pilate (*resolving to be firm*) Now, Claudia, we've had enough of this! I want to hear no more about it. This is hysteria; you *must* control it.

Claudia (*starts to go, then half turns*) I've seen him, you know. He is a good man.

Pilate Where the deuce have you seen him?

Claudia On the Temple steps. I just happened to be passing. I stopped to listen for a moment. They were hurling questions at him from all directions. He stayed calm, he didn't get angry, but his answers were razor sharp and clever. He made them look so small. He's witty, too, a frightening man—you'd only have to look at him, to know . . . he's *good*.

Pilate (*cynically*) Good-looking, you mean?

Claudia Yes—he was that, too.

Pilate And young?

Claudia Oh yes—young.

Pilate That's it, then. You've fallen for the fellow. I've heard all the women chase after him.

Claudia It wasn't like that at all. There's something quite different about him. I wouldn't dare to think of him in that way.

Both Claudia and Pilate look a bit mystified at the implications of what she's just said. Pilate takes refuge in a grunt. At this point in comes Rufus, a centurion who is pro-Jew. He has lived in Israel for many years; oddly enough he likes Jews. In his district he has even built them a Synagogue

Rufus Sir! The High Priests are here with the prisoner . . . and . . . sir?

Pilate Well?

Rufus I know I'm speaking out of turn, but I know the prisoner. He is a fine young man. He did a strange thing; he made a servant of mine who was very ill, better, and he didn't even see him.

Pilate Blessed Jupiter! Not you, too! The lot of you are bewitched! Well, I'll tell you this; he'll have to be pretty bewitching to compensate for getting me up this time of the morning. Go and bring him in. You'd better be off, Claudia; let's hear no more of this nonsense.

Claudia I beg of you—remember!

Claudia exits. Jesus is brought in by the same Temple Guards. He is preceded by Caiaphas, Annas, Joseph, and Judas, who has somehow got in. Rufus has with him another centurion, Scipio, but he is anti-Jew. Jesus looks tired and untidy and he has blood on his head and face and is in chains. A few of the Temple Guards had enlivened the night hours by thoroughly beating him up. In this scene there are no smiles from him—reality has come into its own. Even so he has immense, stern, dignity. (There could be a Jewish crowd off stage, held back by a centurion, who comment with boos, cheers, etc.)

Pilate *(curt)* Well, sirs, I received your dossier. I have looked at it. What do you want me to do?

Caiaphas One thing only . . . ratify the death penalty.

Pilate Not so fast! That is the extreme penalty the law allows. I am not altogether satisfied on the evidence you offer. I am not a Jew, thank God, and I have no time for your taboos and superstitions. They sent me here as a soldier and administrator to preserve order, not as a witch doctor to scare away your ghosts.

Caiaphas *(very cold)* He is a proven enemy of Rome.

Pilate *(no patience with them)* Where are his armies? Where are his swords? When I look at him, I don't hear the crumbling of the Roman Empire.

Caiaphas You have no choice but to eliminate him. He threatens, and rivals the power of Caesar.

Pilate You said that before. In what respect?

Caiaphas He claims to be a king.

Pilate Does he indeed? Well, he looks more like a king than some whose names we won't mention. But a king has a kingdom. What are you, sir? King of the Jews?

Jesus Are you saying that because you really want to know or because they put it in your head?

Scipio gives him a good thump across the head

Scipio Be civil when you talk to the representatives of Divine Caesar!

Pilate *(sharp)* That was not necessary. Save your blows for criminals and degenerates, there are plenty of those about. *(Kindly)* Have you no statement to make in your own defence?

Jesus shakes his head. He has had a beating and is very tired; he cannot muster enough energy to tell this Roman that come what may his own people will kill him

Caiaphas He opposes the payment of taxes to Caesar and his teaching is causing discontent and confusion.

Judas That is a lie! He has said nothing treasonable against Rome!

Pilate Oh? That's unusual for a Jew! May I ask what *is* his attitude towards Rome!

Judas He disregards it.

Pilate (*surprised*) Now, that's clever of him! How can one disregard so vast and efficient an organization in one's own back garden, as it were?

Judas He says it will pass. All things will pass.

Caiaphas (*furious*) I must insist that this man be removed. At first he offered himself as a witness, then he refused to testify.

Judas (*shouting*) Someone must defend him if he won't defend himself!

Pilate Well, if you want to stay, stay, but don't keep shouting out! My head won't stand it this time of the morning.

Annas If he were not a criminal, we should not have brought him before you.

Pilate You have yet to prove to *my* satisfaction that he is. If you think otherwise, deal with him yourselves!

Annas You are fully aware that we are not allowed to put a man to death, not even a man of our own race in our own country.

Caiaphas We are warning you in time of a very serious revolutionary threat in your territory centred round this man. If it grows out of all proportion, *you* and not us will be answerable to Caesar.

Pilate (*angry*) If you're trying to convince me that your main interest here is to preserve *my* good name in Rome, you can save your breath. There's more here than meets the eye. (*Pilate stands in front of Jesus, looks at him; Jesus returns his look unperturbed*) Well, they've certainly got it in for you, haven't they? What have you done to them? What have they got against you? In fact, my young friend—why are they so *frightened* of you?

Protests and indignant noises from Priests

Jesus If I were a threat to anyone, my friends would have fought to save me from arrest in the first place.

Judas (*bawling*) That's true!

Pilate Well, then?

Jesus (*very tired*) You won't understand this—I don't know why I bother— I am here to bear witness to truth, that is why they are afraid.

Pilate (*exasperated*) Great Jupiter! What is truth? I'm not here to discuss philosophy! Look! I find no case against him. If you must satisfy your sadistic impulses, give him a flogging and let him go.

Yells of "No!" from Jewish faction

Rufus May I make a suggestion, sir?

Pilate It must be constructive, and it mustn't take time. I want my breakfast.

Rufus We're going to crucify Barabbas today. Now, there's a real revolutionary for you! The crowds have been shouting for his release all night. Give them Jesus instead!

Caiaphas and Annas protest jointly and loudly, "No, that won't do at all! We won't accept it. He's much more dangerous than Barabbas", etc.

Pilate (*absolutely fed up*) What do you want me to do with him?
Caiaphas (*coldly*) Crucify him!
Pilate (*very disturbed, ponders, then makes one more appeal to Jesus*) Look! I know things aren't always what we think they are . . . (*For Pilate that is a great intellectual conclusion*) Who are you? Where have you come from? Don't tell me what I've already got written down here. It isn't enough to explain this animosity against you. I don't like it. I'm a great advocate of fair play. (*There is quite a silence*) Do you *refuse* to explain yourself to me? (*Shouting*) For God's sake, man, do you know I can pronounce sentence of death? Do you know I have the authority to release you, or to crucify you?
Jesus (*very stern*) You would have no authority at all over me, if I had decided otherwise. (*Long look at Pilate, for whom he is suddenly sorry*) Don't be afraid, the guilt is not yours, it is theirs who brought me here.
Pilate (*very upset and trying to conceal it*) Have you ever seen a man die on a cross?
Jesus Yes.
Pilate It's not a pretty sight.
Jesus No.
Pilate (*turns from him abruptly, barks at Scipio*) Fetch me a bowl of water and a towel.
Scipio (*looking stupid*) Water, sir?
Pilate May the Gods pity me! I am surrounded by knaves and half-wits, and the only *man* I've met for many a long day I'm told to condemn. (*Roars*) A bowl of water and a towel!
Scipio Yes, sir.

Scipio scuffles off

Pilate (*to priests*) You do this on your own responsibility. I find no wrong in him, no case against him.
Caiaphas If you let this man go, you are no friend of Caesar. Any man who claims to be a king is defying Caesar.
Pilate Oh, not again! Spare me these repetitions!
Judas Fools! He has said again and again that his kingdom is not of this world; *in* it may be, but not of it.
Pilate More conundrums! Enough is enough!
Judas Take care. You may do something for which there can be no forgiveness.
Annas If it wasn't for you, he wouldn't have been here in the first place!
Judas I was wrong—*wrong*! I will cry it aloud before all Israel.

Scipio comes back with the water and the towel, places them before Pilate

Pilate Now then, listen to me, all of you. I wash my hands . . . and dry them, so, and at the same time, I absolve myself of any part in what is to follow! I will not be responsible for shedding the blood of an innocent man. Proceed, if you insist, in the usual manner. Scourge him if you must, crucify him if you wish, but—but (*shouting*) remember! I call heaven and earth to witness against you this day—they are *your* orders, not mine!

Pilate goes to the balcony and shouts to the crowd

Who am I to release to you, Barabbas or Jesus?

Crowd (*off stage*) Barabbas, Barabbas!

Pilate What am I to do with Jesus?

Crowd Crucify, crucify, crucify!

Judas (*yelling*) They have planted men in the crowd to stir up feeling against him, they have paid them well! Money's no object to them, they have no scruples! They paid them!

Annas (*cynically*) As we pay all our friends.

Pilate Come. I want to enjoy the privacy of my apartments. I can do nothing more for you. Scipio! My breakfast!

Judas and Jesus exchange a long look. They all exit, and Pilate is left sitting on his chair, sunk in gloom and self-criticism. Suddenly he lifts his head, and listens, there is the faint sound of many voices, "Suffered under Pontius Pilate. Suffered under Pontius Pilate. Suffered under Pontius Pilate."

BLACK-OUT

SCENE 2

The afternoon of the same day. The road to the Cross. The slope of the hill overlooking Calvary. John is supporting the mother of Jesus, who is inarticulate with grief. With them is Mary Magdalene; her sorrow and anger are more voluble

John Are we going all the way?

Mary M. I can't. (*She becomes inarticulate*) . . . The nails . . . into his flesh. (*She shudders*)

John We'll stay here, then . . . later, we'll go and stand by him.

Mary M. I hope it will be over soon.

John The Roman centurion, the kind one, said sometimes they live for as long as three days.

Mary M. (*whispered horror*) Oh God! (*Then a thought strikes her*) . . . He won't . . . they tortured him . . . Oh God give him peace . . . (*Mary his mother reacts to all this, but says nothing*) Can't we do anything?

John It's too late.

Mary M. I wish God would strike them dead.

John I wish Peter was here, or Thomas; they're tougher than us.

Mary M. Don't talk to me about Peter! He's as bad as Judas. Ashamed of him, after all he's been to him. I would never have believed it—and where are the others?

John (*deeply ashamed*) I don't know. I suppose they couldn't bring themselves to stand by and watch.

Mary M. (*scornfully*) Don't make excuses for them! You know they're scared for their own skins.

There is a continuous background of crowd noises and of movement; occasionally people pass to and fro. No one takes any notice of this pathetic little group. Sometimes there's the sound of laughter. A child leads a small group, saying, "Come on! Hurry up, you'll miss it".

Look at them! Just look at them! You'd think it was a picnic! What is it to them! Nothing! They can't even weep for him. Human nature makes me sick!

John Hush, Mary! This does no good.

Mary M. How can you be so calm? Why aren't you fighting, and cursing, and killing? You're a man, aren't you!

John I'm beyond despair. I've accepted it. What else is there?

Mary M. (*shouting*) Well, I can't! Do something! Somebody do something!

Two bystanders pass

He's dying because he thinks you're worth dying for, and look at you!

Bystander What's all the fuss? The bloody Romans crucify someone every day of the week. It's their favourite outdoor sport, nearly as good as the arena. A wise man keeps his mouth shut.

He exits

Mary M. (*in despair*) They don't know, do they? They just don't know!

John It's getting very dark. Why is it so dark?

Mary M. The heavens mourn for him; they're ashamed of humanity. Oh Jesus!

John (*firmly*) We'll say the prayer he taught us—"Our Father who art in heaven," etc.

They go through it to the end, Mary Magdalene in tears; Mary his mother, only her lips move. As they come to the end of it, Rufus enters

Rufus (*gently*) You're his mother, aren't you? His eyes are searching the crowd continually. He's looking for you. Will you come? (*She nods her head, but can't speak*) I'm so sorry. What can I say? He was a fine boy. I spoke up for him you know. I admired him. I never met anyone who talked like him.

John (*matter of fact*) How could you? The truth of God was in him.

Mary M. Oh don't, you're already talking about him in the past! (*She sobs*)

Rufus Don't cry, my girl. I don't know how to put this, but even now I can't be sorry for him; you'd be surprised how much in command of himself he is. Come and see.

Mary M. I'm crying because I'm ashamed to be alive . . .

Judas rushes in, sees the Roman uniform, grabs his arm

Judas You! You're the soldier who tried to save him. Can't you stop it? You! (*To Mary Magdalene*) You can bribe the guards if anyone can. It's still not too late, we'll take him home, nurse him by the sea.

The two women and John shrink from him

Rufus Nobody can do anything now, son; it's as good as over.
Mary M. (*to Judas in a whisper*) I hope you rot in hell!

Judas takes a step towards John

John Keep away, Judas, I'll kill you if you come any nearer.

Judas, stricken, holds out his hands to Mary the mother, and for the first time she speaks

Mary My son is the one who knows how to forgive. (*She turns from him*)

> *Judas sits down on a boulder, head in hands. Rufus leads out Christ's mother. Mary Magdalene and John start to go, but once more she stops and bursts out*

Mary M. No! I can't! I can't face it. I'll have to stay here! I wish I was dead.

John takes hold of her hands and talks to her like a little child. Judas, on his boulder mutters to himself; the last few days have unhinged him somewhat

John Listen, Mary. He went into this with his eyes open. He said to us last night—Oh God, was it only last night? "Nothing, nothing can separate you from me . . . nothing can take you out of the reach of God's hands." He knows what he's doing. If he can stand it, we can.
Mary M. But why, John? Why?
John (*simply, not preaching*) He had to. This way they can't touch him, they can't corrupt him, they can't change him. He is what he always was.
Mary M. (*heartbroken—more moving perhaps if said quietly*) This is no comfort to me. I want him back as he is. I love him, John. I love his eyes, his smile, his voice; these are the things they're killing and these are the things I love. He is my life; there is nothing beyond him.
John (*the penny finally drops*) Mary!
Mary M. Yes?
John In court—you lied, or at least you didn't tell the whole truth . . . (*Pause. She doesn't answer*) You *are* in love with him.
Mary M. (*pause*) Yes. I love him—all the ways one can. I'm not ashamed of it. I thought it might make things worse for him if I said so. (*Bottled-up emotions now released*) Do you think he loves me? I could stand anything if . . .
John (*again a long pause*) The way I see it is this. Love for God and compassion for suffering humanity has wiped all selfishness out of him; that's why he's different from us. So if he loved you that way, he'd think it was

selfish to indulge in it. So many have made such great demands on him. But I'll tell you this. I'm *sure* about this, if it was anybody it would be you!

Mary M. (*whispering*) My darling! My love! I'm ready now, John; I can face it. I want to see him again.

They go out slowly

Judas (*muttering*) Fools, what do they know about it? They don't know the ache in their whole bodies I have in my little finger for him. What do they know about love? Love is a fire! A consuming, terrible fire, a furnace! It destroys, it kills, what it loves, what it wants . . .

A couple of centurions come in, Flavius and Proclus, they mop their brows, take out their lunch, sit down—they don't see Judas, or don't appear to

Flavius Curse this blasted heat! My clothes are sticking to me.

Proclus There's a storm coming . . . thunder about.

Flavius It went dark suddenly, didn't it? I'll be glad to get back to the barracks.

Proclus They're not dead yet.

Flavius I know. Scipio says we're to finish them off. Poor bastards! I never get used to it.

Proclus Degrading business, isn't it? Crucifixion! Sorts them out . . . most of them turn nasty . . . it takes so long . . . they spit out all the filth they know . . . I'm usually at the receiving end . . . I've had my share of death-bed curses. (*He eats as he talks*)

Flavius Yes, or they cry like babies and yell for mercy, and crawl to you in words that sicken the heart. Some of them even scream for their mothers . . . degrading's the word.

Proclus He didn't.

Flavius What are you talking about?

Proclus The Nazarene. He upset me. There I was, bashing away with this mallet and he said . . .

Flavius Well . . .

Proclus He's a nut, he said, "Father, forgive them, they don't know what they're doing" . . . it shook me!

Flavius Poor devil. What did he mean?

Proclus How do I know? He upset me.

Flavius (*laughing*) Upset you? A flaming Jewish criminal getting what he deserved, and he upset you?

Proclus (*curt*) He looked at me as though he was sorry for me.

Scipio comes in carrying a robe over his arm

Scipio Come on, lads! We'll put an end to their misery . . . Jewish Sabbath at sunset. (*Cheerfully*) . . . bloody hypocrites!

Proclus That Jesus—is he dead?

Scipio No, I wish he was. I can't look at him. He's so bloody self-controlled, it's inhuman, not natural. Sends a shiver down me. He's a mighty queer carpenter . . . There he is in mortal agony and won't yell out . . . it's just not natural. I don't like it. Mind you, the others are making enough row for the three.

Flavius (*getting up, collecting his bits and bobs*) What's that you've got?

Scipio His robe. Good bit of material, no seams in it. Wonder where it came from?

Flavius Who's having it?

Scipio We'll draw lots. Come on, lads, let's get it over with.

Flavius and Proclus exit. Scipio lingers for a moment as Judas suddenly comes to life

Judas Don't go! Don't leave me! (*Shouting*) You've got to stop it! He's innocent! You've got the wrong man. (*Suddenly very confidential*) I'm the guilty one. (*Shouting*) It can't end like this!

Scipio You want to bet, pal? Let this be a lesson to you. Respect your betters!

Judas (*most unbalanced*) I've been with him three years, you see, three years. It's quite a long stretch in a man's life. I was with him in the beginning, by the Jordan.

Scipio Pity you didn't both stay there. Watch you don't end up the same way. Well, I'm going to put your friend out of his pain—merciful lot we Romans! Are you coming to watch? Eh? We finish them off with a spear . . . no? You're not coming?

He exits, still cheerful

Judas (*muttering very fast*) Oh, God! Oh, God! Forgive me! I didn't mean it. Don't let him die! Do something. Oh, God of Abraham, Isaac, and Jacob—do something—not this. I'm nobody—nothing—he's different.

*It is almost dark. Judas is on his knees. He hears the voice of Jesus quite clearly**

Jesus Judas! Judas! Why? Why? When no power in heaven or earth, in life or death, could have separated you from me, did you, you of your own free will do it?

Judas I can't live without you. What have I done to you?

Jesus It's all right, son, don't be afraid. No one takes my life from me, I lay it down myself. Don't be afraid. What's done is done, it's over . . .

*AUTHOR'S NOTE. Jesus may be seen at this point—at the back of the stage in white. It has been done this way, and the result was very dramatic, unexpected, and effective.

Jesus exits in the darkness

Judas lifts his head. As usual the personality of Jesus has exorcised the evil spirit. From now on there is a complete and marked transformation in Judas. He stands up and speaks quietly but deliberately

Judas I shall follow you . . . no one can stop me following you. You can die on the other side of the hill there, but I shall find you . . . I shall see you before any of them, before Peter . . . before John.

Rufus re-enters looking tired and unhappy, looks at Judas; there is a slight pause

Rufus He's dead.
Judas I know . . . did he say anything?
Rufus A couple of things. (*He looks uneasy*)
Judas Yes?
Rufus He told his friend to look after his mother.
Judas What else?
Rufus (*pause*) He asked God why he'd abandoned him.
Judas (*quietly*) He did that?
Rufus Yes—none of us thought he'd break . . .
Judas (*grabs hold of him urgently*) What did he say? His words . . . his exact words.
Rufus He called out loudly—he shouted—you must have heard him.
Judas (*impatient*) What did he *say*?
Rufus He said, "My God, my God! why hast thou forsaken me?" (*He is very upset*)

Judas looks distraught, thinks a second and then suddenly laughs out loud. Rufus looks at him as though he's mad

Judas That's all right, then! It's one of our Psalms. King David's Psalms . . . funny how they said he had no time for the law and Scriptures, he could quote it *all*, reams of it, when he wanted to . . . That Psalm, it opens like that, but only the beginning . . . One of the great hymns of our faith . . . Triumph, triumph all the way . . . (*Quotes to himself*) "Though he slay me yet will I trust in him . . . into thy hands I commend my soul!"
Rufus (*excited*) Yes—that's it, that's it, that was the last thing. There was this mighty shout, then a clap of thunder, it was deafening, then he said, "*Into thy hands I commend my soul*", and died. The thunder was like a great voice in the middle.
Judas (*laughing again*) Calling to each other across the universe!
Rufus (*in an urgent whisper*) Who was he?
Judas (*thoughtful, slowly to himself*) Imagination stirred in darkness and a dream was born . . . and he said "Let there be light!" and there *was* light. That is what you and I have crucified today, my friend. We crucified a dream. (*The awful implication strikes him*) A dream in the mind of God!

---

58   The Word and the Flesh

Rufus (*bewildered*) They told me you were the clever one!
Judas . . . not clever enough by half . . .

Scipio, bawling, reappears

Scipio Rufus! Come on! We're off!
Rufus Right. (*To Judas*) I don't understand all this, I wish I did. It's a funny thing, though—for the last few minutes you've been reminding me of him.

Scipio and Rufus exit

Judas is left alone on a very dark stage, quite sane now, but oddly exultant

Judas Where are you? (*Louder, his voice echoing round the stage*) *Where . . . are . . . you?* There's nothing more for me now, is there? I'm—coming to find you! Where are you? . . .

BLACK-OUT

AUTHOR'S NOTE. The play could very well end here. The following scene is an optional extra, and it is left to the individual producer to decide whether or not to use it. If it is used the play ends on a note of hope and new strength, with the disciples standing up and promising to go out and carry on the Christian work.

Thomas walks on

Thomas So that's how it was. Have you ever been sick in your stomach with misery and apprehension? That's how we were that night. Nothing to live for, nowhere to go. The thought of him . . . humiliated, degraded . . . We didn't blame Judas any more; he had the sense to put an end to it. Only, it turned out not to be the end. On the Sunday morning the women went to the tomb to do the usual things, but when they reached it he wasn't there . . . his body had gone. They came rushing back with all sorts of tall stories about young men who looked like angels and a strange gardener who looked like *him*. Although I was frightened, I couldn't take them seriously. You know what women are! Mary particularly, she'd been very hysterical lately. But then something else happened. Peter and the Zebedee boys went home to Galilee. We were short of money and they had to go fishing. In the morning, as they were coming in, they saw him walking along the beach to meet them, he had made a fire and was waiting for them. Well, I wasn't going to believe it, it was too far-fetched, and we decided to meet in the room where we spent that last evening and talk about it. And quite suddenly—now you can believe *me*, can't you?—he was there! Just as usual, no doubt about it, same eyes, same smile, same voice! I started to cry—I don't mind admitting it—I started to cry. I said, "I don't believe it, I *can't* believe it—let me touch you!" And he said, "Come here, Thomas!" and that finished me. I knew who he was then. Mind you, I'd known all along, but I had to say it—I owed him that, I said (*whispers*) "My Lord and My God!"

The lights come dimly up to reveal the kneeling disciples and Jesus

Jesus Peter! Do you still love me?
Peter (*humbly*) Yes, Master, I'm sorry!
Jesus That's in the past. Do you still love me?
Peter Yes, Master.
Jesus Think, Peter, before you answer. Are you sure you love me?
Peter (*heartbroken*) Yes—you *know* I do.
Jesus Then go out into the world and tell everyone, Jews and Gentiles, the things I told you—and, Peter!
Peter Yes?
Jesus No hate! No fear! Love one another!

Peter bows his head

John (*as a calm statement of fact*) We cannot go on without you.
James You saw what happened to us when you left us.
Mary M. Don't leave us again. Never leave us. We can't be what you want us to be when you're not with us.
Jesus Yes, you can. It will be different this time.
John Don't abandon us.
James No; don't forsake us.
Jesus I have told you, I shall never forsake you.

Peter Well, stay here with us. Don't leave again.
Jesus (*patiently*) I shall never leave you.
Peter But it won't be the same if we can't see you!
Thomas Yes, we need to *see* you.
Jesus Whenever you need me, you will find me. When two or three have
   come together in my name, I shall be there. I promise you this, I shall be
   with you always, to the end of the world.

Slow dim to black-out and

CURTAIN

AUTHOR'S NOTE. In the original production the last few bars of the Hallelujah
Chorus were used to end on.

FURNITURE AND PROPERTIES PLOT

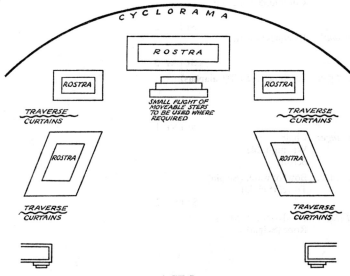

ACT I

Scene 1

On stage: Three large, low tables. *On them:* wine jugs, goblets, bowls, fruit, bread, etc.
Couches
Pile of cushions and rugs
Lyre (one of the girls)

Off stage: Wine jug **(Mary)**

Personal: **Shadrach:** knife
Salome: bangle

SCENE 2

On stage: Stools
Sewing **(Mary)**

Off stage: Towel **(Jesus)**

SCENE 3

On stage: Stools
Large fishing-net
Sandal **(John)**
Table. *On it:* empty food bowls, etc., bowl of figs

SCENE 4

Personal: **Annas:** small purse of money

ACT II
SCENE 1
On stage: Table. *On it:* remains of a meal
           Bread in basket
           Communal wine cup

SCENE 2
Personal: **Disciples:** swords

SCENE 3
On stage: Parchment scroll **(Caiaphas)**

ACT III
SCENE 1
On stage: Chair
           Writing-table
           Scrolls
Off stage: Bowl of water **(Scipio)**
           Towel **(Scipio)**
SCENE 2
Off stage: Food for centurion's lunch
           Robe **(Scipio)**

LIGHTING PLOT

To open: stage in darkness

ACT I SCENE 1

Cue 1	As curtain rises *Flood stage with warm, interior lighting*	(Page 1)
Cue 2	At end of scene *Black-out*	(Page 11)

SCENE 2

Cue 3	When ready *Fade to interior candlelight, with storm outside*	(Page 11)
Cue 4	At end of scene *Black-out*	(Page 16)

SCENE 3 As **Thomas** strolls on to stage

Cue 5	*Spotlight on* **Thomas**	(Page 16)
Cue 6	**Thomas:** ". . . that day in Bethany." *Fade up to warm evening light*	(Page 17)
Cue 7	At end of scene *Black-out*	(Page 25)

SCENE 4

Cue 8	When ready *Fade up to interior lighting*	(Page 25)
Cue 9	At end of scene *Black-out*	(Page 29)

ACT II SCENE 1

Cue 10	As **Thomas** comes on to stage *Spotlight on* **Thomas**	(Page 30)
Cue 11	**Thomas:** ". . . the night I shall remember for ever" *Fade up to interior candlelight*	(Page 30)
Cue 12	At end of scene *Black-out*	(Page 33)

SCENE 2

Cue 13	When ready *Fade up to exterior night*	(Page 33)
Cue 14	**Jesus:** ". . . There's not been enough time . . ." *Light from torches*	(Page 34)
Cue 15	At end of scene *Black-out*	(Page 36)

64   Lighting Plot

SCENE 3

Cue 16   As **Thomas** comes on to stage
            Spotlight on **Thomas**
            Thomas ". . . if you could call it a trial."   (Page 36)

Cue 17   *Fade up to interior candlelight—bright*   (Page 36)

Cue 18   At end of scene   (Page 46)
            Black-out

ACT III SCENE 1

Cue 19   As curtain rises   (Page 47)
            Fade up to early morning light

Cue 20   At end of scene   (Page 52)
            Black-out

SCENE 2   When ready   (Page 52)

Cue 21   *Fade up to cold daylight—dim*

Cue 22   **Mary Magdalene:** ". . . and look at you!"   (Page 53)
            Fade down lighting gradually

Cue 23   **Scipio:** ". . . no? You're not coming?"   (Page 56)
            It is now almost dark

Cue 24   **Judas:** ". . . I'm nobody, nothing, he's different" (Page 56)
            Soft light on **Jesus** *at back of stage*

Cue 25   **Jesus:** ". . . What's done is done, it's over . . ." (Page 56)
            Light out on **Jesus**

Cue 26   At end of scene   (Page 58)
            Black-out

EPILOGUE

Cue 27   As **Thomas** walks on   (Page 59)
            Spotlight on **Thomas**

Cue 28   **Thomas:** ". . . My Lord and My God!"   (Page 59)
            Fade lighting up slightly

Cue 29   At end of scene   (Page 60)
            Slow dim to Black-out

EFFECTS PLOT

ACT I Scene 2

As scene opens   (Page 11)
Effect of violent thunderstorm outside

Cue 1   **Mary:** ". . . except to get thoroughly wet again."   (Page 11)
Blinding flash of lightning and very loud clap of thunder
Storm stops

ACT III Scene 2

Jesus: ". . . What's done is done, it's over."   (Page 56)
One loud clap of thunder